Environmental Science Activities
Handbook for Teachers

Environmental Science Activities

Handbook for Teachers

Bette J. Del Giorno
Millicent E. Tissair

Parker Publishing Company, Inc.   West Nyack, N.Y.

Library of Congress Cataloging in Publication Data

Del Giorno, Bette J
    Environmental science activities.

    Includes bibliographies.
    1. Ecology--Study and teaching (Secondary)
I. Tissair, Millicent E.   joint author.
II. Title.
QH541.D44   301.31'07'12   74-20560
ISBN 0-13-283275-5

Dedication

To our families

How This Book Will Help You Use the Environment as a Laboratory

The environment is the laboratory and the laboratory is the environment. As you and your students investigate your natural and man-made surroundings, you will be making decisions about the quality of the land, air, water, and everything in or on it. No one escapes the environment. It is everywhere and always with us.

This book offers a large variety of practical ways in which teachers and students can investigate the environment together from a scientific and ecological viewpoint. There are many social, economic and political implications to environmental studies and sound scientific investigations must lay the foundation for solutions to these problems.

Each chapter provides demonstrations and experiments related to the study of urban environments, suburban environments, air, water, plants and animals. The environment becomes the laboratory and the teacher sets the stage so the students can discover on their own. The book will be most useful as a handbook of practical activities for classroom use.

In the first chapter, you are told how to use the urban school surroundings to begin studies of the environment. You will learn how to take the students on field trips in the neighborhood to observe the area in its totality and to examine significant nooks and crannies along the way. You will be able to show students how to continue their investigations in a scientific and systematic manner. You will also be able to show them how to study rodent, spider, fly, ant and pigeon populations; the quality of city life; or life in a rain puddle, gutter or on the window sill. These are studies of practical value to the student because they are all a part of his own environment. Furthermore, all these studies will have an effect on the individual and on his own way of life.

The suburban environment includes different things than those found in the urban environment but the investigative techniques are the same. You may wish to study environments at the zoo, in lawns, woods, fields, rivers, streams, lakes, the ocean or in the backyard. The environment is here, there, and everywhere and the approach to studying the fascinating world around us will not differ greatly from area to area.

For example, you will be able to capitalize on the unique experiments for the study of the air, water, and the land. There are several demonstrations and diagrams for examining clean air and for detecting polluted air. The equipment, supplies and materials that are recommended are simple and not difficult to obtain. Students should be encouraged to design their own equipment and build their own materials as an integral part of the experimental process.

The section on the study of water also includes diagrams and experiments that will aid in the investigation of clean water and ways to examine the water for evidence of contamination. Field trips provide on-site experience for the students to observe and collect samples for further testing.

Although the study of land can be a complicated matter, the section dealing with this topic includes tests and experiments that would be quite feasible in most schools. Land forms are studied, soundings are taken, land profiles are charted, and rocks are classified. Soil is tested for its water content, water holding capacity, perculation rate and mineral content.

In the chapters on the study of plants and animals, the activities are divided into two categories. The first considers sampling techniques, plotting microhabitats and ecosystems, keeping records, and studying specific plants and animals. The second category deals with the interaction of plants and animals in their environment.

When the student knows something about interaction and the influence of plants and animals on one another and the role each plays in the community, he can concentrate on populations, communities, and ecosystems. Practical techniques for studying populations, communities and ecosystems are given.

Although years ago it was recommended that the environment be studied as a part of the science curriculum, its importance was not fully recognized and understood until recent years. Now, in view of present conditions, environmental studies are critically needed. The thrust of the environmental crisis is brought out clearly in Chapter 12.

This handbook will provide you with the necessary tools for conducting many worthwhile studies that will ultimately help students enhance the personal quality of the environment for every individual.

Bette J. Del Giorno
Millicent E. Tissair

ACKNOWLEDGMENT

We wish to express our sincere appreciation to Sylvia D. Schmitt for typing portions of the manuscript.

Contents

3. THE AIR WE BREATHE *(Continued)*

4.   EXAMINING THE AIR WE BREATHE 51

5.   WATER—OUR MOST VITAL RESOURCE 69

5. WATER–OUR MOST VITAL RESOURCE *(Continued)*

9. GUIDELINES FOR SOIL STUDIES *(Continued)*

1

Effective Ways to Study
the Urban Environment

PRACTICAL REASONS FOR STUDYING THE ENVIRONMENT

If a man were to lock himself in an air tight closet, he would soon die from his own pollutants. He would use up the available oxygen and increase the amount of carbon dioxide. And so it could happen in the closed system of earth. There is only a limited amount of oxygen in the atmosphere and if we continue to use it up without preserving the oxygen-producing plants on earth, we may suffocate from our own pollutants. It is also possible that if man continues to contaminate our water resources without realizing the potential danger of polluting the fresh water areas and also of filling the oceans with sewage, garbage and radioactive wastes, there will not only be a lack of water to drink, but we will have destroyed the most productive breeding grounds for potential food and oxygen production on this planet. Furthermore, as the human population increases, there will be less land upon which we can grow crops, graze cattle or house people. If man disregards the mounting environmental crisis, he will succumb to suffocation, thirst, starvation or disease. Environmental studies are vitally important because we must find ways to avoid self-destruction. By studying small samples and a limited number of problems, it is anticipated that students will want to adjust their behavior toward a better life. There is much decay evident in the cities. What can we do as individuals and as a group to improve the quality of living in the urban centers? What do our studies tell us and how can we apply what we have learned?

KEY POINTS

Key Points and Activities

Environmental studies are necessary for environmental literacy.
Environmental literacy is essential for intelligent human action.
Environmental action is vital for man's survival.
List other reasons why the study of the environment is important.

HOW TO INVESTIGATE THE URBAN ENVIRONMENT

Let's start where we are—in the classroom—and practice sharpening our senses of seeing, hearing, touching, smelling and tasting things around us. Have the students list what they see in the classroom and record the sounds that they hear. Encourage students to describe the texture of materials, how things feel to them, and tell them to try to identify the materials of which things are made, such as their desks, the walls, chalkboard, chalk, erasers, windows, clothing and so on. Have them keep a notebook and describe the odors they smell and the food they eat during the day for about one week. In order to carry out any significant scientific study, students must be able to describe and to record what they learn through their senses.

KEY POINTS

Key Points and Activities

Learn through the senses:

Taste
Touch
Smell
Sight
Hearing

Record observations made through the senses (TTSSH):

Taste	*Touch*	*Smell* (*Odor*)	*See*	*Hear*
sweet	Texture:	pungent	size	Sounds:
sour	smooth	sweet	shape	Noise—Music
bitter	rough	putrid	color	soft
salty	soft	fresh	texture	loud
metallic	hard	etc.	etc.	high
etc.	etc.			low
				shrill
				dull
				etc.

WHERE TO TAKE FIELD TRIPS TO BEGIN STUDIES OF THE ENVIRONMENT

Since the environment is all around us, we should become aware of our immediate surroundings first before we venture out of the classroom, down the hall and out of the building. Keep in mind that we want the students to use their senses and to record their observations accurately. Students may wish to study other areas of the building or the building itself. They may want to study the schoolyard, the playground, the cracks and nooks in the building or in the pavement, a dirt area or a patch of green grass. The field trips might extend to the sidewalk and gutter, to a junkyard, an alleyway, along a main street, to a vacant lot, a zoo, a transportation depot, or anywhere else in the neighborhood. Ask the students questions to guide them so that they might discover on their own. What are those objects? What properties do they have—color, shape, size, texture? What materials are they made of? What objects or living things are interacting with one another? What evidence is there that interaction is taking place? What things or objects go together? How are things alike or different? The list of questions is endless. Listen for clues from student comments and questions, and pursue their interests. Don't hesitate to inquire with the students. Everyone can have fun and learn together.

KEY POINTS

Key Points and Activities

Field Trips—

Total environment is the laboratory.
Begin where you are.

Make observations of—

Objects and living things.
Properties of objects, and characteristics of living things.

Materials of objects.
Interaction and evidence of interaction.

Objects: anything that takes up space and has mass.
Living things: anything which carries on the life functions of eating, breathing, and can reproduce to bear young like the parent or parents, and also takes up space and has mass.
Properties: characteristics of objects and living things—what something looks like (shape, color, size, texture) observable through the senses.

Material: what something is made of—(wood, metal, stone, flesh, fur, feathers, etc.)

Interaction: when something does something to another which results in evidence of change e.g., when one car hits another, there is interaction between the cars. The evidence of interaction would be the dents.

LOGICAL STEPS FOR SCIENTIFIC INVESTIGATIONS

After a general survey of the surroundings and some experience in observing and reporting, the student should be ready for more specific studies of greater depth. Students may use the Research Team Approach to Learning (ReTAL) and work in teams of two, three, four or, if they prefer, they may work alone. The first step is to help a team of students or individuals select and define the environmental problem they wish to study. The second step is to give the students some background information about the topic they have selected so that they have enough data to continue their studies without your constant guidance. The third step is to provide them with books, articles, films, slides, filmstrips and other visuals to study, or tell them where they are available (as in the media center or library). Suggest that the students interview resource people or invite them to class. If there is a museum or library nearby, make arrangements for them to visit. Be sure the students know why they are going to the museum or library and that they know what questions they want answered. Encourage them to find out as much as they can on their own, but be prepared to redirect them if they should go astray from the main problem they are studying. Once the students have sufficient background to carry out their investigations intelligently, help them set up their procedures. Suggest that one person be responsible for recording all observations. This can be done by keeping a written notebook, taking photographs or motion pictures, drawing, using a tape recorder, making video tapes or by using a combination of one or more of these recording methods. Students may want to make their own filmstrips by drawing directly on film. Later, these records can be presented to the class by the students as a part of their research report.

Many students seem to have a difficult time stating exactly what they mean orally, pictorially or in writing. Help them describe their findings and differentiate between what is a finding (result or what is *observed*) and what is a conclusion (*interpretation* or alternative reasons for the results). Try to keep the studies simple and with as few variables as possible. Provide ample opportunities for students to share their findings and to discuss relationships of one phenomenon with another. More questions may be posed which can provide a natural springboard for a new topic of study. Welcome the new challenge as a means of keeping the curriculum open-ended.

KEY POINTS

Key Points and Activities

Scientific Investigations (work as a team or individual):

1. Deductive process—Background information—Teaching by teacher.
2. Confrontation process—Gathering data from resource materials and persons—Independent studies by students.
3. Experimental process—Designing laboratory activities and performing tests by students.
4. Evaluation process—Discussing findings and conclusions with team members and sharing knowledge gained with class—Teaching by students.

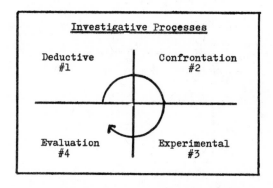

OBSERVING LIVING THINGS

Students may wish to focus on a study of the rodent population in a back alley, habits of a spider living in the school basement, the fly population in a trash barrel, an ant population in a crack in the schoolyard pavement, the pigeon population in the peak of the building or man himself living on that block. The life in a rain puddle, the gutter or on the window sill can also reveal ecological relationships as well. Encourage the students to find topics of interest to them.

Living things include plant and animal life. Ask the students to look for different kinds of plant life in and around the school. They may find indoor plants, ivy, grass, weeds, barberry bushes, trees and numerous other plants striving to survive in the cracks of the sidewalk or pavement. Even if the students do not know the name of the plant, have them draw it and label one "A," another "B," and so on. Later, they can try to identify the plants using a key. Count the number of plants that are the same withing a defined area—say one square yard (or one square meter)—within the schoolyard, the school block or the park across the street. Count the number of different plants. How many are flowering plants? Which ones stay green all year around? Why do some plants grow in certain places? Are certain plants only found in shady areas? How is it that plants have the strength to grow up through sidewalks and pavements?

Encourage students to respect living things and to beautify the classroom and school grounds by planting and caring for plants.

KEY POINTS

Key Points and Activities

Living things behave in certain ways.
Select an animal or plant population to study:

1. Observe living habits—dwelling, food gathering, courting, relationships with one another, other animals, plants and the physical environment—describe (Chart No. 1).
2. Select and mark off a defined area for plant studies (Chart No. 2).

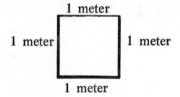

a. Count number of different plants.
b. Count number of plants that are the same.
c. Examine location for soil texture, pH, water content, amount of sunlight. (See subsequent chapters for directions, especially Chapter 9.)
d. Consider reasons for certain plants growing in certain places.

HOW TO ADAPT ENVIRONMENTAL INVESTIGATIONS TO CONDITIONS IN THE URBAN COMMUNITY

Although there may not be much vegetation around the school, a small patch of green is all that is needed to study the numbers and kinds of plant and animal populations in a community. In fact, population studies can be carried out in a corner of the schoolyard, in

Name of animal under study _____

Observations--Week Beginning: _____

	Day 1	Day 2	Day 3	Day 4	Day 5
1. Dwelling, habitat, location, material					
2. Food gathering					
3. Courting					
4. Relationships with each other					
5. Relationships with other animals, plants					

Chart 1

Plant Plot: Location _____ Size _____

Observations—Week Beginning: _____

	Day 1	Day 2	Day 3	Day 4	Day 5
1. No. of different plants					
2. No. of plants that are the same (refer to 1 above) "A" _____ "B" _____ "C" _____ "D" _____ etc.					
3. Soil textures (sandy, gravel, clay, loam)					
4. Soil pH (Acidic, Basic)					
5. Soil water content					
6. Amount of sunlight (number of hours per day shining on plot)					
7. Plant growth (inches or centimeters) "A" _____ "B" _____ "C" _____ "D" _____ etc.					
8. Notes—Why do certain plants grow in certain places?					

Chart 2

a vacant lot or in a crack in a sidewalk. A patch of hard-packed dirt can be compared to a desert; a hedge to a forest.

Soil profiles can be studied at construction sites where foundations are being dug or highways are being constructed. Students can gain insight as to how mountains, valleys and plains were formed by observing the gullies fashioned by water eroding the soil as it flows from drain pipes. Students can speculate how riverheads are formed and how soil is deposited by watching the water run off after a rain storm or by simulating a river in a soil or gravel bank. Students can study rocks and minerals by examining the building materials of which the school is constructed. Are the stairs made of the same composition as the walls? What is brick? Where does it come from? What is marble, granite, concrete, cement?

Have students look for evidence of decay and deterioration. What happens to old cars, trash and garbage? What happens to the plants and animals that die? Can you see evidence of chemical changes taking place in, for example, old cars rusting, garbage cans rusting, buildings rotting away, surfaces of statues wearing?

Perhaps there will not be a pond or stream available for water studies but this should not deter you from such attempts. If you want a sample of "fresh" water, collect rain water in a plastic container. This may have particulate matter in it but would be more like fresh pond water than tap water which has chlorine, heavy metals and perhaps fluorine in it. Rivers in the city may all be encased in concrete or metal pipes. You can use these sewers, drainage canals, rain water gutters and drain pipes as examples of what happens to the water and the surrounding land when the natural meander of a river is altered and straightened. Again, if there is a patch of land anywhere in the schoolyard, the students can build a meandering river and one that has been straightened and compare the differences. Why should we not be allowed to fill in and build on the flood plains?

If you can take the opportunity to examine the water in a freshly made puddle right after a rainstorm, you will have an artificial fresh water pond. If you want to study the water in a stagnant pond, find an abandoned tire or a discarded can where water has collected. After you have taken your water samples, turn over the tire or the can. Living organisms should be abundant under them. These objects can substitute for a fallen log and a rock respectively.

Other animals, common in the city, that can be studied for behavior patterns and relationships with other living things and the physical environment are the starlings, sparrows, and, of course, the pigeons. Caution the students, however, not to bring in dead birds. They often carry viral diseases. There should be worms in the ground too, and if not, the students might investigate the reasons for their absence. How does the available food supply relate to the kinds of animals you find in your area? All animals need food and shelter. Does the school environment provide these necessities for life?

With a little imagination, almost any investigative experience can be adapted to the conditions which exist in an urban community. For specific determinations, refer to subsequent chapters.

KEY POINTS

Key Points and Activities

Adapting environmental investigations to the urban community:

Study Plants	—house plants, plants growing in sidewalk cracks, in a vacant lot, in a corner of the schoolyard.
Study Land	—a patch of hard-packed dirt can be a simulated desert; a hedge row can be likened to a forest; soil profiles can be made at construction sites; rocks and minerals can be studied in construction materials.
Study Water	—rain drains, gutters and pipes become rivers; puddles, tin cans, old tires provide ponds.
Study Chemical Changes	—look for evidence in rusting trash, decaying garbage, rotting buildings, worn surfaces of statues.
Study Animals	—birds, pets, rats, cockroaches, flies, spiders, worms—for behavior and population studies.

GLOSSARY

conclusion — an interpretation, or alternative reasons given for the results.

finding — a result, or what is actually observed.

interaction — when something does something to another which results in evidence of change e.g., when one car hits another, there is interaction between the cars, and the evidence of interaction would be the dents.

living things — anything which carries on the life functions of eating, breathing and can reproduce to bear young like the parents, and also takes up space and has mass.

material — what an object is made of—(wood, metal, stone, flesh, fur, feather, etc.)

object — anything that takes up space and has mass.

properties — characteristic of objects and living things—what something looks like (shape, color, size, texture), observable through the senses.

ReTAL — Research Team Approach to Learning, an investigative process including the inductive, confrontation, experiment and evaluative phases.

BIBLIOGRAPHY

Del Giorno, Bette J. "The Research Team Approach to Learning (ReTAL): A Structure for Open-Endedness" *Science and Children.* Vol. 6, No. 6, March 1969.

Pollock, George F. *The Conservation Story.* Columbus, Ohio: American Education Publications, 1969.

Science in City and Suburb. Staff of *Current Science.* Columbus, Ohio: American Education Publications, 1969.

2

Methods for Studying the Suburban Environment

LOOKING FOR DIFFERENT THINGS IN THE SUBURBS

Consider yourself fortunate if you live in the country—for pollution problems in the suburbs are not as great as they are in the cities, at least, not yet. You may still be able to take a walk in the clean woods, romp through an open field, investigate a marsh, swim in a clear pond, or just relax amid the flowers and trees in your own backyard. If you look a little closer, however, you will discover evidence of deterioration in the quality of your environment. You don't have to look very far to find litter—everywhere—beer cans, soda bottles, waste paper and styrofoam cups. The skies are not quite as clear as they used to be for the air carries with it pollutants and tiny particles blown in from industrial areas. The water too shows signs of man's presence. By dumping chemical and human waste into our rivers and lakes, the water becomes unfit for swimming, to say nothing of drinking it. The places where our parents and grandparents fetched spring water hardly exist anymore and the old swimming hole has vanished.

You will want to have your students begin their environmental studies in the classroom as in Chapter 1. Have them practice sharpening their senses and recording accurately. Give them an opportunity to express themselves and help them to be specific in their descriptions. From the classroom, they can move into the school building and then out to the schoolyard. Extend the laboratory into their homes and into their own backyard. Discuss such questions as "What is the environment?" It is important for the individual to realize that the environment is everything around him and that he is influenced continuously by his surroundings, hence it is to his advantage to learn as much about the environment as possible.

There are things you will find in the suburbs that you will not find in the city. You will find many more lawns for instance, and a lawn can provide interesting studies of plant, insect and worm populations. Depending upon the area in which you live, you may be able to study the sea, seashore and estuaries, streams and rivers, lakes and ponds, freshwater marshes, the desert, the tundra, the grasslands or the forest at first hand. These areas comprise the major ecosystems of the world. An *ecosystem* is a system which includes the *biotic* community (living organisms) and the *abiotic* (nonliving) environment.

KEY POINTS

Key Points and Activities

Areas found in the suburbs:

classroom	lake
schoolyard	pond
backyard (lawns, gardens)	marsh
sea	desert
seashore	tundra
estuary	grassland
stream	forest
river	

Record observations and discuss.

Ecosystem—a biotic and abiotic functional unit, or the cyclic energy flow from producers to consumers and to decomposers.
Biotic—living organisms (plants, animals and protists).
Abiotic—nonliving environment (elements and compounds).
Producers—autotrophic organisms (green plants).
Consumers—heterotrophic organisms (animals).
Decomposers—microconsumers, saprophytes, or heterotrophic organisms (bacteria, fungi).

SELECTING PLACES FOR FIELD TRIPS

If you want to give the students some experience in planning research projects in the field and in learning what to look for and how to record observations, a field trip to the zoo can be an instructional and motivating device. The ecology of Africa, from where many of the animals in the zoo come, is an extremely important study today because Africa has one of the last frontiers not disturbed by man. If there is a film on Africa available, show it to the students prior to their in-depth studies.

Before the class goes on the trip, find out which African animals are at the zoo. Have each students or a team of students choose an animal to study. Have them look up such basic questions as the following:

1. What does the animal look like?
2. To which *Class* and *Order* does the animal belong in the *Kingdom* Animalia?
3. Where does the animal live? Where does he make his nest or home? How does he build his home?
4. How does he gather food? What does he eat?
5. How does he choose his mate? How many offspring does he usually produce?
6. What is the estimated population of this animal in the wild? In captivity?
7. What natural enemies does this animal have?
8. What laws, if any, protect this animal?
9. What would happen to the ecosystem of which this animal is an integral part, if he should be eliminated?
10. What would happen to the economy of Africa and our own economy if this animal were to become extinct?
11. Discuss what is meant by a *food chain,* a *food web,* an *ecosystem* and the *balance of nature* as it relates to the animal you have chosen.

After the above search, the students should be able to list some other questions they can have answered when they visit the zoo, for example:

1. How well has the animal adapted to his new environment?
2. How long can he usually survive in captivity?
3. How does his cage compare to his natural home in the wild?
4. What does he eat in the zoo as compared to his diet in the wild?
5. How does his behavior in the cage compare to his behavior when he was free to roam?
6. Are the young produced in captivity as frequently, or as infrequently, as they are in the wild?
7. What is the purpose of having animals in a zoo? Are the reasons justified?

The last question suggested above is a good one for class discussion.

When the students have completed their studies, have them share what they have found and encourage them to use pictures, drawings, diagrams, charts and other illustrative materials to make their presentation clear and interesting.

A trip to a pond, whether fresh water or marine, offers a good introduction to field study. Here, students can study the basic components of a small ecosystem: the elements and chemical compounds of the water, the green plants or producers (autotrophs), the animals or consumers (heterotrophs) and the microconsumers and decomposers (saprophytes) such as bacteria and fungi. Group students in teams and let them select an assignment to study. Have them collect and run tests on one of the components above. One team can concentrate on the chemical composition of the water: collect water samples, find the density, determine the turbidity, odor and color, measure the pH (acidity and alkalinity), calculate the rate and direction of water flow, and test for dissolved oxygen (DO). Specific directions on how to conduct these studies are outlined in Chapter 5. Students will also want to look for evidence of pollution—fecal, chemical and thermal. Directions for these tests are given in Chapter 6.

A second team of students may wish to collect *plankton* (tiny, free-floating plants and animals) and estimate the number of *phytoplankton* (tiny plants) per square meter (m^2) and determine the amount of chlorophyl there is per square meter of phytoplankton. Chlorophyl can be extracted with acetone. Chlorophyl is an indicator of the food producing potential at a given time since it reacts to the available nutrients, temperature and light.

Other teams can study the larger green plants and sea weeds, or the animals in and around the pond, or the bottom populations of decomposers. You will need a good compound microscope with an oil immersion lens to see the microorganisms since most of them are not visible unless magnified about 1,000 times. More information on studies like these is included in Chapter 7.

In the fall, an old garden, or a grass or weed covered field can be used as a simple terrestrial (land) ecosystem. Teams working in threes can study the plant and animal populations within a specified area. Some teams can study the plants; other teams, the animals. A third group can study the interrelationships between animals, and a fourth group can observe the relationships between plants and animals. A sharing of the information among teams can interrelate the studies and present a total picture.

Field trips can be taken to the ocean, the shoreline, an estuary, a coral reef, a stream or river, a lake, a fresh or salt water marsh, a swamp, a bog, a desert, a grassland, a forest or the tundra. Each area has unique characteristics and is vitally important to the balance of nature in the biosphere. The ocean is a source of food and minerals and the estuaries are the nurseries of the world. More food and oxygen are produced in the estuaries than anywhere else. On the seashore, one can see the transition from water plants and animals to land forms. A stream or river is a living system and a link to the sea. A coral reef is one of the most complete ecosystems known. A marsh, swamp, or bog acts as a giant sponge to hold back flood waters. A desert or the tundra offers many examples of special adaptations made by organisms to survive in these regions. The forest is rich in illustrating the interdependence of living things.

A field trip, just out-of-doors, can be an exciting adventure. Plan specifically what you want to look for. Give students the ground rules before you go, and go out into the laboratory to explore.

KEY POINTS

Key Points and Activities

Field trips to

zoo
pond
garden
grass or weed covered field

Make observations of—

animals from Africa—compare life in captivity with life in the wild.
ecosystems—acquatic and terrestrial.
pond—elements and compounds, producers, consumers, decomposers.
field—(land)—plants and animals.

Components of an Ecosystem

1. Abiotic Substances—elements and compounds.
2. Producers—Autotrophic (able to produce their own food) organisms, i.e. green plants.
3. Macroconsumers—large heterotrophic (eat other living things) organisms, i.e. animals.
4. Decomposers and Microconsumers—tiny saprophytic (eat dead organic matter) and heterotrophic organisms, i.e. bacteria and fungi.

Food Chain: the transfer of energy from plants to animals to larger animals with repeated stages of eating and being eaten (green plants are eaten by animals and animals are eaten by other animals).

Food Web: branched food chain where many more predators will eat a particular prey thus making a simple food chain complex.

Balance of Nature: the dynamic interrelationships of plants, animals and the environment that tend toward equilibrium if not disturbed by an outside force.

HOW TO DETERMINE WHAT TO STUDY

One of the first things you will want to do is to find out what resource people are available and which resource facilities are in your area. For example, if there is an agriculture experiment station, the Audubon Society, Sierra Club, conservation commission, college or university, bird sanctuary, fish hatchery, and the like in your vicinity, find out who the specialists are and how you might coordinate programs with them. Don't overlook your town government officials because they have many contacts and are usually very willing to help. Make this an assignment for your students too. Meanwhile, outline your course or the environmental unit you wish to teach based on what you have learned about the community. Present the outline to your students and discuss it. Encourage them to plan the curriculum with you and participate in designing laboratory exercises and field trips. They may have more to contribute than you realize.

Keep in mind that environmental studies are not limited to ecology or biological sciences. Although this book attempts to give you some practical ways to test and evaluate the quality of the environment from an ecological viewpoint, it in no way means to deny that environmental education covers all disciplines. Therefore, in order to have a balanced viewpoint, students must consider the aesthetic, cultural, sociological, economic, and political aspects of environmental problems. Pollution is the result of man's flagrant disregard for the totality of the environment and the role he plays in the scheme of nature. Up until recently, man has felt a need to conquer nature in order to survive; now he must readjust and learn to live with nature in order to survive, for he is not a part *from* nature but rather, a part *of* it.

So as to focus on the interdisciplinary nature of environmental studies, you may wish to use a problem oriented approach and consider the various aspects of the problem. For example, you and your students may wish to survey your community and identify existing or potential problems. Suppose one of the problems noted is an alga bloom on a small pond. The students can look into the history and formation of the pond to see if its chronological age corresponds to its eutrophic age. When a pond is young, it has low nutrient content and is said to be *oligotrophic,* having few living things in it. As it ages, more nutrients are added and thus, more living things can be found in it. It is then called an *eutrophic* pond. However, if the pond has a superabundance of nutrients including nitrates and phosphates, eutrophication becomes excessive and an *alga bloom* results. Thus the pond becomes "suffocated" by too much plant life.

After appraising the stage of development of a pond, the students can begin looking for the source(s) of excessive nutrients—mainly phosphates and nitrates. They should ask such questions as: Does farmland border the pond and do the farmers use fertilizers containing nitrates and phosphates? Is the water becoming contaminated by means of fertilizer running into the pond, or is the fertilizer getting into the underground water? Are detergent wastes containing phosphates draining into the pond or into a feeder stream? If the students can trace the contamination to the source, they should then ask "What can be done about it?" In considering alternative solutions, be sure the students investigate the consequences of any action from political, economic, engineering and aesthetic viewpoints. Moreover, the ideal solution may not be the most realistic, and many alternatives should be considered.

Curriculum will grow out of the interests, needs, background, and experiences of the students if you encourage their participation in planning the unit or course. Another approach to determining what to study would be to select together what you think are healthy environments and compare them to those you decide are unhealthy. Students can develop a set of characteristics or attributes present in a good quality environment and a set for those environments considered of poor quality. Further studies would focus on the degree of quality from good to bad. Tests can be run on the specific components, results compiled, and conclusions drawn. When the ecological data has been collected and the facts are known, you and your students can proceed knowing you are doing so based on scientific findings, and not on emotion or political propaganda. Your class will become alive with enthusiasm and interest because they will be working on real problems and will be discussing current and vital issues.

KEY POINTS

Key Points and Activities

Resource facilities and people—

Agriculture Experiment Station
Audubon Society
Sierra Club

Conservation Commission
College or University
Bird Sanctuary
Fish Hatchery
Town Government Departments   1827136
etc.

Plan Curriculum Together—teacher and students.
Environmental Studies include all disciplines, and aesthetic, cultural, sociological, economic and political aspects must be considered.
Man must learn to live as a part of nature in order to survive.
Oligotrophic—stage of pond development where few living things are present due to lack of nutrients.
Eutrophic—stage of pond development where many living things are present due to an abundance of nutrients.
Alga bloom—an excess amount of algae growth on fresh or marine bodies of water resulting primarily from an overabundance of nutrients—mainly phosphates and nitrates.

APPROACHES FOR STUDYING THE SUBURBAN ENVIRONMENT AND ITS IMPORTANCE

A study of the suburban environment is important, not only because of its impact on living things of the area but also because it offers a site for comparison. Moreover, healthy environments still exist in the suburbs and preventative measures can be taken before irreparable harm is done. Knowledge of the ecological factors can provide the basis for making decisions regarding what will happen to our environment in the future.

All approaches to environmental studies, then, should be scientific, practical, and reflect an awareness of future consequences. What may appear to be good today may prove to be disastrous over a period of time, as we have found to be the case with some pesticides. The individual must first become aware of his surroundings. Then, through a series of experiences, he should be better able to evaluate the quality of the environment. Subsequently, he should be able to separate the good from the bad, work at correcting the bad, and predict what will happen as a result of his modifying the environment. A simple example of how this approach can be carried out follows.

Ask the students to go out-of-doors and collect objects from the environment and bring them into class. When they return, ask them to build something with the objects, create an art object, write a poem about them or whatever they wish. Encourage them to use their imagination. Ask them what objects they have found and have them interpret what they have done with them. Ask them questions similar to these:

1. How many of you found beer cans? How many were found altogether? (Write the number on the chalk board.)

2. How many plastic containers did you find? (Write the number on the chalk board.)

3. What else did you find and how many of each? (Record.)

4. What would happen to the beer cans, plastic containers, etc. that you found if they were to remain where you found them? Are they picked up and brought to a dump? Do they disintegrate or just pile up? How can we find out? (Experiment.)

5. What does all this tell us about our society?

6. Which of your objects do you think make your environment better? Worse? Give some reasons for your decisions.

7. What did you do with your objects? What message are you trying to convey with your representation?

8. How would you describe an environment of good quality?

9. What can man do to correct the conditions you have observed in order to improve the environment? If some action is taken to correct what you have identified, what do you think might happen in ten years?

10. If no action is taken to correct the situation or situations you have identified, what do you think will happen in ten years? Is your prediction based on scientific evidence? Explain.

The specific techniques for studying the environment are essentially the same for the suburbs and the city.

KEY POINTS

Key Points and Activities

A study of the suburbs is important because—
Studies of suburban environments offer a comparison with urban environments. Give several comparisons.
The environment affects every individual. Give several examples.
Some suburban environments can be saved from further deterioration. Discuss ways in which this can be accomplished.
Approaches to studying the suburban environment should be scientific, practical and reflect an awareness of future consequences.
Techniques for studying the suburban environment should not differ greatly from techniques for studying the urban environment.

GLOSSARY

abiotic — non-living, refers to the environment containing elements and compounds.

alga bloom — an excess of algae growth on fresh or marine bodies of water resulting primarily from an overabundance of nutrients, mainly phosphates and nitrates.

autotrophs — organisms that make their own food—live on inorganic matter.

balance of nature — the dynamic interrelationship of plants, animals and the environment that tends toward equilibrium, if not disturbed by outside forces.

biogeochemical cycles — the more or less circular paths of the chemical elements passing back and forth between organisms and environment.

biotic — refers to living organisms (plants, animals, protists).

carnivore — an animal or meat eater.

ecological succession — (1) it is the orderly process of community change; these are directional and therefore, predictable; (2) it results from the modification of the physical environment by the community; (3) it culminates in the establishment of as stable an ecosystem as is biologically possible on the site in question.

ecology — the study of the structure and function of ecosystems or nature. There are five basic levels of organization: (1) organism; (2) population; (3) communities (biotic and abiotic); (4) ecosystems (energy flow of organisms and non-living environment); (5) biosphere (the portion of the earth where ecosystems can operate).

ecosystem — a basic functional unit which includes the biotic community (living organisms) and the abiotic (non-living) environment. There are four constituents of an ecosystem: (1) abiotic substances (elements and compounds); (2) producers (autotrophic organisms—green plants); (3) macroconsumers (large heterotrophic organisms—animals); (4) decomposers or microconsumers (saprophytes—heterotrophic organisms—bacteria, fungi).

eutrophic — stage of pond development where many living things are present due to an abundance of nutrients.

food chain — the transfer of food energy from the source in plants through a series of organisms with repeated stages of eating and being eaten (green plants are eaten by animals and animals are eaten by larger animals).

food web — a branched food chain where many more predators will eat a particular prey thus making a simple food chain complex.

habitat — the place where an organism lives (address).

herbivore — a plant eater.

heterotrophs — organisms that must eat other living things—live on organic matter.

microclimate — local conditions of temperature, light, etc.

niche — the role the organism plays in the ecosystem (profession).

oligotrophic — stage of pond development where few living things are present due to the lack of nutrients.

saprophytes — plants that break down complex compounds of dead protoplasm, absorb some of the decomposition products and release simple substances; also heterotrophs, that decompose dead organic matter i.e., fungi, bacteria.

trophic level — in complex communities, organisms whose food is obtained from plants by the same number of steps are said to belong to the same trophic level—based on function:
first trophic level — green plants (producers)
second trophic level — plant eaters (herbivores) (primary consumers)
third trophic level — carnivores that eat herbivores (secondary consumers)
fourth trophic level — carnivores that eat carnivores (tertiary consumers).

BIBLIOGRAPHY

Odum, Eugene P. *Ecology.* N.Y.: Holt, Rinehart and Winston., 1963.

Pimentel, Richard A. *Natural History.* N.Y.: Reinhold Publishing Corp., 1963.

Smith, Robert L. *Ecology and Field Biology.* N.Y.: Harper and Row, Publishers, Inc., 1966.

Wentworth, Daniel F., J. Kenneth Couchman, John C. MacBean and Adam Stecher. *Pollution—Examining Your Environment.* Minneapolis, Minn.: Mine Publications Inc., 1971.

Yasso, Warren F. *Oceanography—A Study of Inner Space.* N.Y.: Holt, Rinehart and Winston, Inc., 1965.

3

The Air We Breathe

This chapter will be helpful to you in providing the proper experiences for your students when they perform the activities in Chapter 4.

AIR, WEATHER AND POLLUTION

Weather, at any given time, controls the amount and location of pollutants in the air. *Pure air* is a mixture of gases—21% oxygen, 78% nitrogen, .03% carbon dioxide, less than 1% argon, and traces of other gases. In the natural state, air also contains some water vapor and particles coming from forest fires, decaying matter and active volcanoes. Although the earth's atmosphere is many miles high, about 95% of the air mass is concentrated in a layer only 12 miles or 19.31 kilometers thick around the crust. The *troposphere,* the lowest part of the 12 mile or 19.31 kilometer layer, ranges from 5 to 10 miles or 8.045 to 16.09 kilometers thick only and contains the air necessary for life. It is indeed a limited atmosphere yet we continue to fill it up with atmospheric garbage where it remains until some natural force in the weather removes it.

Impress upon your students that the main elements of weather are sunshine, temperature, wind, air pressure, and moisture. The atmosphere responds to the sun and its energy. The sun's energy warms the air in three ways: by radiation, conduction and convection. As the sun *radiates* heat and light, this energy is transferred to the earth, is absorbed by the land and water, and is reradiated as heat energy. *Conduction* is the transfer of heat by the physical contact of molecules of air and the warm earth. *Convection* is the rise and fall of air masses as they are heated and cooled. Warm air expands and rises; cool air contracts and sinks. These forces can mix and dilute pollutants in the air and cause them to rise or fall to the earth. The same phenomenon is true in water. Warm water rises, cold water sinks.

Solar radiation, conduction, convection and the earth's rotation are responsible for wind formation. The sun's energy is absorbed and reflected according to the type and topography of the earth's surface. The more energy reflected, the less energy absorbed. The heat holding capacity of the earth's surface (specific heat) differs according to the composition. For example, land areas heat faster than water and will rise to a higher temperature but water will retain its heat longer than the land. These factors have an affect on surface winds causing them to move in different directions. As the earth rotates, the air currents form prevailing winds which can stabilize, mix or disperse the air pollutants.

Air pressure is an important factor in trapping pollutants and stabilizing their movement. When a high pressure mass of cool air is at the earth's surface and a warmer low pressure mass of air is over it, the cool air can not rise and take away the pollutants. This condition is called an *inversion.*

When water vapor condenses in the air, it forms fog. The warmer the air, the more moisture it can hold. Fog can also hold small particles of matter which form a screen shutting out the sunlight. The water in fog can also dissolve carbon dioxide and sulfur dioxide to form carbonic acid and sulfurous acid respectively. Atmospheric acid has played a role in nearly all our major air pollution disasters.

KEY POINTS

Key Points and Activities

Air is a mixture of gases:

21% Oxygen (O_2)
78% Nitrogen (N_2)
.03% Carbon Dioxide (CO_2)
less than 1% Argon (Ar)
traces of other relatively inert gases
water vapor
organic particles

Troposphere—extends outward from the poles about five miles (8.045 kilometers) and 10 miles (16.09 kilometers) at the equator; it is the inner part of the 12 mile (19.308 kilometers) layer of air surrounding the earth's crust.

Main elements of weather:

sunshine   air pressure

temperature   moisture
wind

The sun warms the air in three ways:

radiation—the transfer of heat and light energy through space.
conduction—the transfer of energy from higher energy molecules to lower energy molecules by direct contact.
convection—the transfer of energy by moving molecules in a gas or liquid, as in the rise of warm air and the sinking of cold air.

Have your student give examples and set up some demonstrations of radiation, conduction and convection.
For instance:
A. *Radiation*
   1. An electric iron radiates heat. When the heat strikes the hand, one feels the sensation of heat.
   2. Light a candle and place a glass chimney over it. Without touching the chimney, can you feel the heat from the flame?
B. *Conduction*
   1. Heat a metal rod in the flame of a Bunsen Burner. Note that the other end soon becomes warm because the molecules of metal have conducted the heat from one end to the other.
   2. Using the candle lamp again, place your hand on the glass. Does it feel warm? Explain.
C. *Convection*
   1. Add some food coloring to ice water and pour it into a beaker of very hot water. You will see the cold colored water sink.
   2. Light the candle once more and place your hand over the top of the chimney but do not touch it. What do you notice? Explain.
D. Ask the students to give other examples and to design similar experiments.

Inversion—the condition which exists when a layer of cool air is trapped below a layer of warm air preventing the bottom layer and pollutants from rising and dispersing.
For discussion:

What specific effects would an acidic atmosphere have on us, other animals and plants?

TYPES OF POLLUTANTS

Each year more than 200 million tons of pollutants, which fall into six main classes, are released into the air over the United States. Transportation, primarily the automobile, is the biggest single polluter, accounting for 42 percent of all pollutants by weight. The automobile produces the major portion of carbon monoxide, hydrocarbons, and nitrogen oxides.

Carbon monoxide (CO) is a colorless, odorless, poisonous gas, slightly lighter than air, and is produced by the incomplete burning of carbon in fuels. Almost two-thirds of all the carbon monoxide comes from internal combustion engines, with the giant portion coming from gasoline-powered motor vehicles. Carbon monoxide emission may be reduced by supplying sufficient air to insure complete combustion. The end-product of complete combustion is carbon dioxide, a natural constituent of the atmosphere.

Hydrocarbons (HC), like carbon monoxide, are the products of unburned and wasted fuel. However, hydrocarbons, at concentrations normally found in the atmosphere, are not toxic but are considered major pollutants due to their role in the forming of photochemical smog. More than half of the estimated 32 million tons of hydrocarbons produced each year come from gasoline-powered vehicles, 27 percent come from miscellaneous burning, and 14 percent from industrial sources. Over 60 percent of all hydrocarbons are found in the urban areas, due to the large number of automobiles.

Nitrogen oxides (NO_x) are produced when the fuel is burned at very high temperatures. Stationary combustion plants produce 49 percent of the nitrogen oxide emissions, transportation vehicles account for 39 percent while all other sources yield 12 percent.

Particulate matter includes particles of solids and liquids which are large enough to see, as fly ash and smoke, to particles too small to be seen without the aid of an electron microscope. Some particulates are so small that they may remain suspended in the air for a long time. They are produced primarily by fuel combustion (31 percent) and industrial processes. Forest fires and other miscellaneous sources account for 34 percent.

Sulfur oxides (SO_x) are acrid, corrosive, poisonous gases produced by burning fuel containing sulfur. The burning of coal produces about 60 percent of all sulfur oxides, oil represents about 14 percent and an additional 22 percent are emitted from industrial processes.

Most of the coal and oil is burned in electric power generating plants. Approximately two-thirds of all the Nation's sulfur oxides are emitted in urban areas, with seven industrial states in the Northeast responsible for over one-half the national total.

Photochemical oxidants are a complex variety of secondary pollutants which are formed when nitrogen oxides combine with gaseous hydrocarbons in the presence of sunlight. These chemical oxidants, together with solid and liquid particles in the air, make up what is commonly known as smog. Some of the pollutants included in this group are ozone (an unstable, toxic form of oxygen), nitrogen dioxide, peroxyacyl nitrates, aldehydes, and acrolein.

KEY POINTS

Key Points and Activities

Types of Pollutants:

1. Carbon monoxide (CO)—from internal combustion engines.
2. Hydrocarbons (HC)—from unburned fuel.
3. Nitrogen oxides (NO_x)—from combustion fuel burned at high temperature.
4. Particulate Matter—from most anything—just small particles suspended in the air.
5. Sulfur oxides (SO_x)—from burning sulfur fuels.
6. Photochemical Oxidants—from the reaction of nitrogen oxides and hydrocarbons in the presence of sunlight.

For discussion:

1. What are some of the other pollutants found in air?
2. Some scientists believe that an increase of carbon dioxide in the atmosphere would result in the "greenhouse effect" forming an artifical ceiling around the earth. What effects would this have on the earth and us? You may want your students to do some research on this.

ANALYSIS OF AIR—CLEAN AIR VERSUS POLLUTED AIR

As was said before, clean air should contain oxygen, nitrogen, a little carbon dioxide, some traces of other gases, and water vapor. Today, clean uncontaminated air is a rare commodity. So much in fact, that some enterprising persons are sealing fresh mountain air in cans and are selling it to tourists! One does not have to be a scientist to determine that something is polluting the air. Just by using the senses, pollution can be detected. There are pollutants, of course, that can not easily be detected, but on the whole one just has to be aware in order to "sense" pollution. Some times you can taste pollution. It may be bitter, metallic or sour. You can touch things and feel the grit, dirt, and soot. Your eyes may smart and water; your throat may hurt and you may cough. You can smell pollution—some odors are faint and others and strong and pungent. You can see pollution in the form of smog, smoke, garbage and litter. You can hear pollution in the rasping noises and shrill sounds of the cities and the endless drone of traffic. Some plants and animals have been able to build up an immunity to the contaminated atmosphere, but unfortunately, many others have succumbed to these hazardous and abnormal constituents of the air we all must breathe. We may still have a choice. What will it be? Discuss this with your students.

KEY POINTS

Key Points and Activities

Observe through the senses:

Taste	Sight
Touch	Hearing
Smell	

For the next few days have the students write down all the pollutants they can detect through their senses.

DETERMINING THE VALUE OF CLEAN AIR TO HEALTH

Dirty air can kill as we have seen in Denors, Pennsylvania, New York City and London. In 1948 in Denors, nearly 7,000 persons became ill and 20 died because of the industrial pollutants trapped over the town. In 1953, 1963 and 1966, New York City reported that over 700 deaths were perhaps due to the smog that hung over the city. On an average day, a person walking the streets of New York inhales an amount of toxins (poisons) equivalent to 38 cigarettes. In London in 1952, the famous "killer" smog was thought responsible for the deaths of 1600 to 4000 people. In 1962, the London smog was blamed for 700 deaths. In each case, weather conditions were such that the dispersion of the pollutants could not occur.

Air pollution contributes to respiratory diseases and shortens our lives. Air pollution contributes to the cause of common colds, bronchial asthma, and pneumonia. Air pollution and smoking are closely linked to chronic bronchitis. Air pollution is associated more and more with the cause of emphysema, the progessive breakdown of air sacs in the lungs, due to chronic irritation. Lung cancer is found twice as often in air polluted cities than in rural areas. The United States proportionally has twice as much lung cancer as Norway where the air is much cleaner. Research has shown a definite correlation between dirty air and the incident of cancer of the lung.

Ask your students if they know the symptoms of air "pollutionitis"? Headaches, dizziness, nausea, irritated eyes, nasal discharge, chest pain, difficulty in breathing, sore throat and coughing—just to name a few. In some instances, a specific pollutant may be responsible for these symptoms. In other instances, it may be a combination of many. When carbon monoxide is inhaled, it displaces the oxygen in the blood and can cause dizziness, headaches and can make a healthy person accident prone. It has been found that if a person breathes air containing 80 parts per million (ppm) of CO in an eight hour period, 15% of his hemoglobin would be affected. This is equivalent to about 1 pint of blood. For persons suffering from anemia, heart disease, thyroid malfunction or lung disease, carbon monoxide can impose an extra burden on them. Cigarette smokers are even more adversely affected. Sulfur oxides, especially sulfur dioxide, can cause severe damage to delicate tissues of the eyes, nose, mouth and lungs. Sulfur dioxide, on contact with water, forms sulfurous acid and sulfuric acid which can cause serious damage to membranes.

Photochemical oxidants, associated with smog, have been related to increased irritation of the eyes and asthma attacks. Particulate matter in the atmosphere amplify the danger to human health. Beryllium and asbestos in the air, for example, can cause lung lesions.

KEY POINTS

Key Points and Activities

Air pollution contributes to the cause of:

common cold	chronic bronchitis
bronchial asthma	emphysema
pneumonia	lung cancer

Symptoms resulting from air pollution:

headache	abnormal nasal discharge
dizziness	chest pain
nausea	difficulty in breathing
eye irritation	sore throat
cough	

Activity—GATHERING RESEARCH DATA

1. Have the students go to the library and search for more information on the topic of air pollution and health.
2. Write to organizations concerned about environmental health such as the American Cancer Society, the Heart Association and the National Tuberculosis and Respiratory Disease Association and ask them to send research reports related to air pollution and health.
3. Discuss the value of clean air for health.

LOOKING FOR EVIDENCE OF DAMAGE DONE
BY POLLUTANTS

The cost of air pollution has been estimated by a Congressional Committee to be close to $20 billion per year. Air pollution interferes with such basic human needs as food, clothing and shelter. It mars our natural beauty and aesthetic objects. It also reduces our safety and disturbs the balance of nature.

Industries producing phosphates emit fluoride compounds into the air which eventually fall to the ground and stunt the growth of or kill citrus trees. It also softens the bones of grazing animals. Sulfur oxides, coming primarily from power plants, form sulfite and sulfate ions which, on contact with water, form sulfurous and sulfuric acid respectively. This can occur on the surface of plants as well as on the mucous membranes and in the lungs of animals—damaging potential food products. Likewise, ozone, a pungent (like garlic), colorless gas present in photochemical smog, does damage to the leaves of plants and to fruits such as strawberries and apples. Ozone also damages the leaves of tobacco plants and some garden flowers. In general, air pollution stunts the growth of shrubs and flowers, injures trees and crops and damages much vegetation. As a result of air pollution, livestock have become ill and farmers have lost a great deal of money, and the average consumer has had to pay dearly for the food that is marketable.

Air pollution soils and rots clothes. In heavily polluted areas, it has been estimated that a household might spend as much as $200 per year per person for laundry, cleaning of drapes, rugs and upholstery, and washing of walls and windows.

Air pollution causes deterioration of our homes. It rusts metals and discolors house paint. It erodes stone, and coal dust can be found on houses and in the yards. The White House has to be washed frequently to remove the soot from air pollution.

The National Gallery of Art and the art galleries in Boston claim air pollution is causing the paintings and other art objects to deteriorate. The primary cause is apparently due to sulfites and sulfates in the air. Monuments, statues and public buildings have become rapidly worn and pitted. In Europe, and especially in London, buildings have had to be sandblasted to get them clean and to restore their beauty. The Library of Congress has reported that the books and magazines stored there are being damaged by air pollution. Nothing seems to escape its effect.

Besides being directly hazardous to our health, air pollution also contributes to accidents. Fog and smog reduce visibility and can cause driving and flying accidents. Air pollution has been the reason for closing airports from flight traffic many times. Studies have also shown that air pollution can disturb the balance of nature. For example, there seems to be a direct relationship between the activities of steel plants in the south end of Chicago and Gary, Indiana and the unusual weather experienced downwind in the town of La Porte. This community has 1/3 more thunderstorms, 1/3 more days of precipitation, and 4 times more hailstorms than any other town within a 15 mile radius of South Chicago and Gary.

KEY POINTS

Key Points and Activities

Air Pollution affects:

food
clothing
shelter

natural beauty
safety
balance of nature

Damage by air pollutants to:

A. Foods
 1. Fluorides
  a. damage citrus trees.
  b. soften bones of cattle.
 2. Sulfur oxides
  a. form acids on plants and animal membranes.
 3. Ozone
  a. damages leaves of plants and fruits.
B. Clothing
 1. Soils and rots fabric, nylons, rugs, drapes, etc.
C. Homes and Buildings
 1. Rusts metals.
 2. Discolors paint.
 3. Covers buildings and yards with soot.
D. Aesthetic objects
 1. Deteriorates paintings, books, magazines.
 2. Wears out and pits monuments, statues and public buildings.
E. Safety
 1. Reduces visibility for driving and flying.
F. Balance of Nature
 1. Disturbs weather patterns.

Activity—LOOKING FOR EVIDENCE OF DAMAGE DONE BY POLLUTANTS

1. Have students choose one of the categories of air pollution damage above (food, clothing, shelter, etc.) and read further on the specific damage done by pollutants. Consider the economic

aspects of the damage and include a section on what can be done to solve the problem. You may wish to use the following format:

Title
Statement of the Problem
Background Information
Economic Aspects
Proposed Solution(s)

2. Have students keep a daily log on all the evidence they find of damage caused by air pollution. Ask them to determine which pollutant or pollutants caused the damage and give reasons for their selection.
3. Go on a field trip around the school with the whole class and make a list of all the damage they think was caused by air pollution.
4. When the students have completed each of the activities above, have them share the information with their classmates. Encourage them to use as many visuals as possible to make their presentations interesting.

PROTECTING YOUR RIGHT FOR CLEAN AIR

Ask your class what is being done to protect your right as a citizen to breathe uncontaminated air? Probably not enough in many areas of the country. Recognition of the need for legislation for control came many years ago. The first federal Air Pollution Control Act was passed in 1955 and declared "that the prevention and control of air pollution at its source is the primary responsibility of state and local governments."

Some state and local governments did pass nominal control programs, while industry continued to move slowly and spend very little of its resources on research, development and installation of pollution control devices.

In 1967, citizen concern brought about the enactment of a more stringent federal law, Air Quality Act, 1967, and citizen concern and involvement is essential for its execution and implementation. This new law is not without its shortcomings but at least it does empower the federal government, through the Department of Health, Education and Welfare (HEW), to take corrective action if the states fail to meet their control responsibilities.

In general, this is the way the Air Quality Act of 1967 works:

1. The HEW designates air quality control regions based on climate, meteorology, topography, urbanization and other factors affecting pollution problems.

2. HEW develops air quality criteria for the major pollutants: particulate matter, sulfur oxides, hydrocarbons, carbon monoxide, etc. These criteria must tell the levels at which these pollutants, individually and in combination with others, are known to have adverse effects on public health and welfare.

3. Upon receipt of the federal criteria, the state must present these air quality standards to public hearings before adoption and to the HEW for review and approval after state adoption.

4. Following approval of the standards by HEW, the state must file a plan for implementation, maintenance and enforcement of its air quality standards.

5. Additional sections of the Act provide for the HEW to step in and establish standards in the event a state fails to meet its obligation.

Each state government should have, in its executive branch, a commission or commissioner who is responsible for the Clean Air Act. Have your students contact him and find out what is being done in your state.

There are also many nationwide volunteer citizens groups who have developed many fine educational materials for use in the classroom. Some of these agencies are:

American Heart Association
American Cancer Society
National Tuberculosis and Respiratory Disease Association

KEY POINTS

Key Points and Activities

Legislation for Control:

Air Pollution Control Act 1955
Air Quality Act 1967

To obtain copies of these Acts write to:

The Conservation Foundation
1717 Massachusetts Avenue, NW
Washington, D. C. 20036

GLOSSARY

carbon monoxide — (CO) —a colorless, odorless, toxic gas produced by the incomplete combustion of carbon fuels such as gasoline, coal, oil, and natural gas.
conduction— the transfer of energy from higher energy molecules to lower energy molecules by direct contact.

convection — the transfer of energy by moving molecules of gas or liquid as in the rise and fall of air and water. Both air and water will expand and rise upon warming and both will contract and fall upon cooling.

inversion — the condition which exists when a layer of cool air is trapped below a layer of warm air preventing the bottom layer and pollutants from rising and dispersing.

nitrogen oxides — (NO_x)—compounds of nitrogen and oxygen formed from fuels burned at high temperatures.

particulate matter — small particles suspended in air because they are too small to settle out.

photochemical oxidants — formed when nitrogen oxides and hydrocarbons react in the presence of sunlight. Some of the oxidants in the group include ozone, nitrogen dioxide, peroxyacyl nitrates, aldehydes and acrolein.

radiation — the transfer of heat and light energy through space.

sulfur oxides — (SO_x)—compounds of sulfur and oxygen of which sulfur dioxide (SO_2) is common. SO_2 is a heavy, colorless gas with a pungent odor formed primarily from burning coal, oil and other sulfur fuels, and also produced in chemical plants, by processing metals and burning trash.

troposphere — the inner part of the 12 mile layer of air surrounding the earth, it extends outward 10 miles at the equator and 5 miles at the poles.

BIBLIOGRAPHY

Connecticut Air Conservation Committee c/o Connecticut Tuberculosis & Respiratory Disease Assocation, Inc. *Needed: Clean Air,* 1970.

Earth Science Curriculum Project, *Investigating the Earth.* Boston: Houghton-Mifflin, 1967.

Eblen, William, and John Dallar, Vivian Dorvall. *Air Pollution: The World's Exhaust.* West Haven, Connecticut: New Age Books Pendulum Press, Inc., 1971.

Kelly, James, and Harold Wengert. *Pollution—Man's Crisis: An Investigative Approach.* Bismarck, North Dakota: N.D. Studies; 1971.

Life Education Reprint #69 *Air Pollution.* New York, 1969.

　　　Life Educational Reprint #92 *Cars and Cities: On a Collision Course.* New York, 1970.

National Air Conservation Commission. *Air Pollution Primer.* National Tuberculosis and Respiratory Disease Association, 1969.

Rienow, Robert, and Leonatrain Rienow. *Moment in the Sun,* New York: Ballantine Books, 1967.

The Conservation Foundation. *Your Right to Clean Air: A Manual for Citizen Action.* Washington, D.C. 1970.

4

Examining the Air
We Breathe

DETECTING PARTICULATES IN THE AIR

BACKGROUND

Particulate matter, or particles which can be found in the air, may be classified as solids, gases or aerosols. Some of the solid material may be soot, ash, soil, or dust. Much of the solid material comes from the incineration of refuse, fires, dust storms and soil erosion. The most prevalent gases are carbon monoxide and sulfur dioxide. These come from incomplete combustion of gasoline, natural gas, burning of sulfur-containing fuels, and smelting and refining of ores. *Aerosols* are insoluble particles suspended in a gas. The particles are too small to be pulled to the earth by gravity and remain suspended in the gas. Many of the garden and household aerosols are potentially dangerous because, if they are not dispersed by a fan or the wind, they can cause respiratory illnesses.

Activity 1: DETECTING NUMBER AND TYPES OF PARTICULATES

MATERIALS *(per class)*

10 Petri dishes or plastic coffee can covers
   white petroleum jelly (Vaseline), silicon grease or glycerin
   graph paper
   tape

METHODS

1. Tape the graph paper to the bottom of each Petri dish or plastic cover. (Figure 4-1).

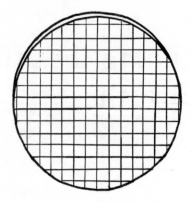

Figure 4-1. Particulate Counter

2. Grease the inside of the dish (or cover) with vaseline or one of the other preparations mentioned above. You now have a *particulate counter.*

3. Place these particulate counters in various places in and out-of-doors.

4. Check the particulate counters each day and record the day you begin to observe particles collecting on the grease.

5. After one week, collect all the particulate counters, making sure you code each counter so you know where it was located.

6. Using a stereoscope (dissecting scope) or a large hand lens, count the number of particles you found per cm^2 for each sample.

7. Count the number of different kinds of particles you find on each sample.

8. Try to identify the types of particles. Do you find any that are magnetic?

9. Return the particulate counters to the same locations and let them remain for another week. At the end of that time, repeat the steps above.

After performing the above activity, your students may wish to try to find out from where some of the particulate pollutants come. Select the particulate counter that is contaminated the most and do the following activity.

Activity 2:   DETERMINING SOURCE OF PARTICULATE POLLUTION

MATERIALS (per class)

10 particulate counters (see Activity No. 1 for construction)

METHODS

1. Make a reasonable guess as to what your particles are and from where most of them come. For example, if there is a gas station nearby, you may predict that many of the particles found on your counter could be coming from there.
2. Make up some fresh particulate counters and ask the owner of the gas station if you can place some of the counters in and around the station. Tape some on the walls too.
3. In a few days, collect the samples and compare them with your original particulate counter. Was your prediction that most of the pollutants came from there accurate?
4. What kind of particulate matter would you expect to find in that atmosphere (gas station)?

Activity 3:   DETECTING PARTICULATE MATTER FROM CAR EXHAUSTS

MATERIALS (per student)

large piece of poster board (oak tag)
large piece of filter paper or paper toweling
glass wool (fiber glass used in aquaria filters, angel hair)
tape

METHODS

1. Roll a piece of poster board to the size which will fit around the exhaust pipe of an automobile. Tape it together to make a tube.
2. Tape a filter paper or piece of paper toweling to cover one end. (Figure 4-2.)
3. Place the tube around the exhaust pipe.
4. Ask the driver to start the car and let it run for one minute.

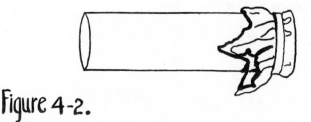

Figure 4-2.

5. Ask the driver to turn off the engine. Carefully remove the tube from the exhaust. Remove the filter paper and examine. If only a few particles have collected, repeat the experiment for a longer duration.
6. Place a clean filter paper on the tube.
7. This time, fill the tube with glass wool to filter the particulates coming from the exhaust.
8. Fit the open end onto the exhaust pipe. Run the car's engine for one minute or for the amount of time recorded above.
9. Remove the tube. Remove the filter paper and examine. Record your observations.
10. Remove the glass wool. What do you notice? How would the use of an exhaust filter affect air pollution caused by automobiles? What are the pollutants of the internal combustion engine?

Activity 4:   ESTIMATING THE DENSITY OF BLACK SMOKE

MATERIALS (per student)

Power's Micro Ringelmann chart—(may be obtained from
    McGraw-Hill, New York, New York)
3" x 5" card
ruler
scissors
pencil

METHODS

1. If the Ringelmann Smoke Density Charts are not available, have the students draw four 1 inch squares along the top of a 3" x 5" card. (Figure 4-3.)
2. Draw a 4" x 1/2" rectangle directly under the squares.

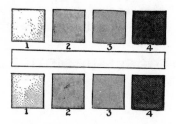

Figure 4-3. Smoke Chart

3. Under the rectangle, draw four more 1 inch squares so they line up with the ones above.

4. Below the squares, label the numbers 1, 2, 3 and 4. The density of the smoke is divided into four categories from light smoke, No. 1, to dark smoke, No. 4.

5. Shade the squares with a pencil. Square No. 1 should be very light gray. Square No. 2 should be darker; No. 3 darker than No. 2 and No. 4 very dark but *not* black.

6. Cut out the center rectangle. You now have a modified Ringelmann Smoke Density Chart.

7. Observe several smoke stacks in your area for a few days. Hold up the Ringelmann Smoke Density Chart and record the date, time, location and number of your Ringelmann Chart. Select the Ringelmann No. that is most like the shade of smoke coming from the stack.

8. Record your observations for at least one week and try to observe at the same time each day.

9. Compute the average Ringelmann number for each stack per day or per week. Add up the Ringelmann numbers and divide by the number of observations you made. For example:

Location stack	A			
Observation No.	1	4	9:00 a.m.	Oct. 1
	2	3	noon	Oct. 2
	3	4	2:00 p.m.	Oct. 3
	4	4	9:00 a.m.	Oct. 4
	5	3	noon	Oct. 5
	6	4	2:00 p.m.	Oct. 6
		22/6 = 3.66		Average

10. Check with your local or state Air Pollution Control Agency. According to your observations, are air pollution standards

being met? What conclusions can be drawn about the efficiency of the operation of the smoke stack sources?

TESTING FOR SULFUR DIOXIDE CONTENT

BACKGROUND

You may want to review some basic chemistry with your students before proceeding with this section.

Sometimes the presence of sulfur dioxide in the air can be detected by its sharp acidic odor; however, its presence in the air can best be discovered by its reaction with potassium permanganate ($KMnO_4$). Potassium permanganate is purple in solution but turns a pale pink in the presence of sulfur dioxide gas (SO_2). The reaction is stated below:

$$2KMnO_4 + 5SO_2 + 2H_2O \xrightarrow{\text{[HCl]}} K_2SO_4 + 2\,MnSO_4 + 2H_2SO_4$$

The above reaction will occur only in the presence of hydrochloric acid (HCl), therefore, a little HCl is added. This reaction will detect SO_2 in the air and can also be used to determine the volume of SO_2 present in the air at a given time.

Activity 1:   MEASURING SO_2 IN THE AIR

MATERIALS (per class)

*0.99% potassium permanganate ($KMnO_4$)(See page 58)
250 ml Florence flask (or boiling flask)
2 hole stopper to fit flask
2 pieces of glass tubing; one piece to reach 1" or 2.5 cm
   below and 1" or 2.5 cm above the stopper, and
   the second piece to reach to the bottom of
   the flask and 1" or 2.5 cm above the stopper
air pump (aquarium aerator)
piece of rubber tubing to connect pump to long piece of glass
   tubing
dilute hydrochloric acid (HCl)
10 ml graduated cylinder
distilled water
100 ml graduated cylinder

METHODS

1. Place the glass tubing in the two hole stopper. (CAUTION: To

prevent glass breaking in your hand, moisten the stopper and glass with water or glycerine and hold in a cloth when inserting.)

2. Pour 100 ml distilled water into a 250 ml Florence flask.
3. Using the 10 ml graduated cylinder, add 1 ml 0.99% $KMnO_4$.
4. Add 1 ml dilute HCl and place stopper on flask.
5. Connect long glass tube with the air pump by means of the rubber tubing. Connect the air pump to a wall outlet and turn on the electric current. (See Figure 4-4.)

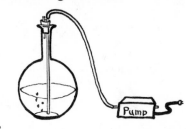

Figure 4-4.

6. Record the time when you turn on the pump. Let the air pump operate until the $KMnO_4$ turns colorless. This may take several hours. When the solution is colorless, record the time and turn off the pump.
+7. Calculate the volume of air pumped through the $KMnO_4$. This can be done by multiplying the number of minutes that the pump was in operation by the pumping capacity of the pump (liters of air per minute). (See page 58.) For example:

$$\text{Volume of Air} = \text{\# of Minutes} \times \frac{\text{Liters of Air}}{1 \text{ Minute}}$$

If it pumped 3 hours at 3 liters of air per minute, then

V of Air = 180 minutes X 3L/minute
V = 180 x 3
V = 540 Liters - the volume of air pumped through the $KMnO_4$ that was needed to decolorize it.

8. Calculate the mass of air—

If 1 L of air has mass of 1.3 grams then 1.3 g x L = _?_ grams.

In the example above, 1.3 g x 540 L = 702 g. We know that 1 g SO_2 is required to decolorize 0.99 gram of $KMnO_4$ and in this experiment, the 0.99% $KMnO_4$ contains .99 g $KMnO_4/100$ ml. Therefore, 1 ml of solution contains 0.0099 g $KMnO_4$.

$$\frac{.99g}{100 \text{ ml}} = \frac{xg}{1 \text{ ml}} \qquad 100x = .99, \ x = \frac{.99}{100}, \ x = .0099g$$

It will then take 0.01 g SO_2 to decolorize 0.0099g $KMnO_4$.

Therefore, the 540 liters of air or 702 g contained a mass of 0.01 g of SO_2. This is enough to decolorize the 0.0099 g of $KMnO_4$ that 1 ml of 0.99% $KMnO_4$ solution contains.

9. How many parts per million (ppm) of SO_2 is contained in a particular volume of air which decolorizes $KMnO_4$? Use this proportion:

$$\frac{xg\ SO_2}{1,000,000\ g\ Air} = \frac{0.01\ g\ SO_2}{Mass\ of\ Air}$$

In the case above, the mass of air was 702 g, $\therefore$

$$\frac{xg\ SO_2}{1,000,000\ g\ Air} = \frac{0.01\ g\ SO_2}{702\ g}$$
$$702\ x = 10,000$$
$$xg\ SO_4 = 14.2\ grams\ of\ SO_2$$

Conclusion: The sample of air tested contains 14.2 parts of SO_2 per million parts of air.

* HOW TO MAKE UP A 0.99% POTASSIUM PERMANGANATE SOLUTION

MATERIALS (per class)

potassium permanganate ($KMnO_4$)
distilled water
250 ml beaker
100 ml graduated cylinder
400-500 ml reagent bottle with ground glass stopper

METHODS

1. Weigh out .99 grams (g) $KMnO_4$ and place in 250 ml beaker.
2. Dissolve $KMnO_4$ with 50 ml distilled water.
3. Pour dissolved $KMnO_4$ into a 100 ml graduated cylinder.
4. Add distilled water up to volume (100 ml).
5. Pour into a reagent bottle and stopper tightly. Label 0.99% $KMnO_4$.

+CALCULATING VOLUME OF AIR DISCHARGED FROM AIR PUMP PER MINUTE

MATERIALS (per student or team of 2 or 3 students)

250 ml graduated cylinder

battery jar or gas collecting trough
water
air pump (aquarium aerator)
air hose
glass plate

METHODS

1. Fill battery jar half full of water.
2. Fill graduated cylinder with water and cover with glass plate.
3. Turn the cylinder over holding the glass plate in place.
4. Place in water of battery jar and remove glass plate.
5. Insert the tubing connected to the air pump into the cylinder while it is underwater. (Figure 4-5.)

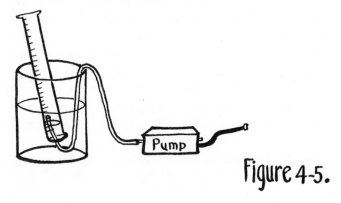

Figure 4-5.

6. Record the time and turn on the air pump.
7. Record the time again when the air has displaced the water in the graduated cylinder.
8. Calculate the volume of air discharged from the pump per minute.

To calculate:

1000 ml = 1 liter, therefore, 250 ml = 0.250 liter.
If, for example, 5 seconds were needed to displace the water in the cylinder by the pump, the proportion would be set up as follows:

$$\frac{x\ L}{60\ seconds} = \frac{0.250\ L}{5\ seconds}$$

$$5 \times L = 15$$

$$x\ L = \frac{15}{5}$$

$$x = 3\ L\ \text{- the volume of air discharged from the pump per minute.}$$

Now return to Activity 1, No. 6.

LOOKING FOR INCREASED AMOUNTS OF CARBON DIOXIDE

BACKGROUND

In a general sense, finding evidence for increased amounts of carbon dioxide is rather difficult. Sometimes one can see evidence along a busy street for the trees may look wilted and yellow. Also, in an atmosphere with elevated amounts of CO_2, one may feel uncomfortably warm and find difficulty in breathing. An uncovered dish of lime water [$Ca(OH)_2$] in the presence of CO_2 will turn a milky white. This is the test for carbon dioxide.

$$CO_2 + Ca(OH)_2 \longrightarrow CaCO_3\downarrow + H_2O$$

The calcium carbonate formed is a white solid precipitate.

Ordinarily there should be 300 parts of CO_2 per million parts of air. Carbon dioxide is essential for the photosynthetic process in plants where food and oxygen are produced by green plants. Some authorities fear that a build up of carbon dioxide is possible and would result in an overall heating of the earth due to the greenhouse effect. Ultraviolet rays and visible light from the sun can penetrate the CO_2 and heat up the earth. It is more difficult for the earth to radiate heat out into space again through the layer of carbon dioxide, therefore the earth's atmosphere remains warm. Increased amounts of CO_2 will cause the earth to warm up more than is normal and some scientists fear that eventually the polar icecaps will melt causing disastrous floods.

Let your students try to measure quantitatively the amount of carbon dioxide in the air.

Activity 1: MEASURING THE AMOUNT OF CARBON DIOXIDE IN THE AIR

MATERIALS (per class)

1.68 g calcium hydroxide [$Ca(OH)_2$]
250 ml Florence flask or boiling flask
2 hole stopper to fit flask
2 pieces of glass tubing; one about 3" long, the other about 18" long
air pump (aquarium aerator)
piece of rubber tubing to connect air pump
10 ml graduated cylinder
100 ml graduated cylinder

1000 ml graduated cylinder
1000 ml beaker
reagent bottles
glass rod
medicine dropper

METHODS

1. Set up the apparatus used for measuring SO_2.
2. Weigh out 1.68 g $Ca(OH)_2$. Set aside.
3. Pour 1 liter (1000 ml) distilled H_2O into a one liter beaker.
4. Add the 1.68 g $Ca(OH)_2$ to the one liter distilled H_2O. Stir with glass rod until dissolved.
5. Pour $Ca(OH)_2$ solution into a reagent bottle and stopper tightly. Label $Ca(OH)_2$ Solution (Lime Water).
6. Pour 100 ml distilled H_2O into a 250 ml flask.
7. Add 1 ml $Ca(OH)_2$ (Lime Water) to the 100 ml distilled H_2O.
8. Add 2 drops of Phenolphthalein indicator solution to the $Ca(OH)_2$ solution in the flask. Solution should turn pink. (Phenolphthalein is pink in base and colorless in neutral or acid solutions.) Set aside.
9. Determine the number of liters of air your air pump pumps per minute as calculated for measuring SO_2.
10. Connect air pump to glass tube in stopper of Florence flask. Record time. Turn on current and allow to run until $Ca(OH)_2$ solution becomes colorless (neutral——►acid).
11. When solution becomes colorless record time and turn off pump.
12. Calculate the volume of air that passed through the solution to cause it to decolorize.
    Volume of Air = # minutes x Liters/minute (capacity of pump)
13. Calculate the number of grams of air from the volume.
    Remember: 1 liter of Air has a mass of about 1.3 grams
    $\therefore$ Mass of Air = Liters x 1.3 grams
14. Calculate the number of parts per million (ppm) of CO_2 in the air.
    Note: It takes 0.001 gram of CO_2 to make the solution colorless
    $\therefore$ set up the following proportion:

$$\frac{X \text{g } CO_2}{1,000,000 \text{ g Air}} = \frac{0.001 \text{ g } CO_2}{\text{Mass of Air}}$$

Conclusion: The sample of air tested contains____parts of CO_2 per million parts of air. Would you expect the concentration of CO_2 to vary in different locations?

SPOTTING OZONE AND NITROGEN OXIDES AS
CONTAMINANTS IN THE AIR

BACKGROUND

Ozone and nitrogen oxides are closely related in air pollution
mainly because as amounts of oxides of nitrogen increase, the amount
of ozone increases. The relationship can be seen in the following
equations:

$$NO_2 \longrightarrow NO \quad + \quad O$$

nitrogen yields nitrate   +   oxygen
dioxide   oxide

$$O \quad + \quad O_2 \longrightarrow O_3$$

oxygen + oxygen yields ozone
gas

Nitrogen oxides, mostly nitrogen dioxide (NO_2) and nitric oxide
(NO_3) are discharged into the atmosphere from motor vehicles at the
rate of about 6 million tons per year. Industry contributes 2 tons each
year. Nitrogen dioxide is a brownish gas at room temperature and is
soluble in water. When it dissolves in water, it forms nitric acid and
nitrous acid.

$$2NO_2 \quad + \quad H_2O \longrightarrow HNO_3 \quad + \quad HNO_2$$

nitrogen   +   water   yields   nitric   +   nitrous
dioxide   acid   acid

Ozone is formed when a single atom of oxygen combines with
oxygen gas. This reaction takes place in the presence of sunlight and
hydrocarbons. The combination of ozone, nitrogen oxides,
hydrocarbons and sunlight produce a photochemical smog. This
condition occurs in areas where there are many industries and
automobiles, where the population is dense, where the climate is
warm, and where there is poor ventilation, as within a valley.

Although one cannot look up into the sky and identify specific
pollutants as being ozone or nitrogen oxides, there are definite signs
that point to the possibility of their presence. Sometimes after a spring
electrical storm, you can detect a faint odor of garlic. This is an indication that there may be increased amounts of ozone. This odor may
also be detected when sun lamps or ultra violet lamps (U.V.) are used
because U.V. lamps produce O_3. The appearance too, of smog on a
warm summer day may be evidence of these photochemical
pollutants. If you make a study of the objects and organisms around
you, such as the plants, rubber products or synthetic fabrics, you may
see them change over a period of time. For instance, pollution can

retard the growth of plants or stop it altogether. Ozone, in particular, causes rubber products to deteriorate, and oxides of nitrogen will cause synthetic fabrics such as nylon stockings to disintegrate, especially if nitric or nitrous acids are formed. Let your students try the following experiments:

Activity 1:   FINDING EVIDENCE FOR THE PRESENCE OF NITROGEN OXIDES

MATERIALS (per student)

empty coffee cans
old nylon stockings and other synthetic fabrics
strong tape
twine

METHODS

1. Wrap a piece of nylon stocking around the open end of a coffee can and do the same with the other synthetic fabrics.
2. Tape the fabric to the can.
3. To be certain the fabric is secure, tie a piece of twine around it too. You now have a *nitrogen oxide detector*. (Figure 4-6.)

Figure 4-6.

4. Make several nitrogen oxide detectors and place them in various areas around the school, in the community and around the home. Be sure to locate some where you can reasonably guess you will find oxides of nitrogen. Code them so you will know where you located a particular fabric.
5. Check your nitrogen oxide detectors every week for three months. Record your observations.
6. After three months, collect all your nitrogen oxide detectors. Code them so you will know where they were located. Record your observations.

7. Examine your samples under a stereoscope (dissecting scope) or a large hand lens. What do you see?
8. Examine particles of each fabric under a compound microscope. What has happened to the fabric? Can you see differences in the durability of the fabric, that is, does one synthetic hold up better than another?

Activity 2:   COMPARING THE DURABILITY OF NATURAL AND SYNTHETIC FABRICS IN A NITROGEN OXIDE ENVIRONMENT

MATERIALS (per student or team of 2 or 3 students)

Natural fabrics:

cotton
wool
silk

Synthetic fabrics:

rayon
orlon
nylon

Nitrogen oxide detectors

METHODS

1. Prepare several nitrogen oxide detectors as described in Activity 1 with the pieces of material listed above.
2. Select a location where you know there is contamination by nitrogen oxides. An area should have been identified in Activity 1.
3. Place the nitrogen oxide detectors in that location. Be sure you have one or more of the following combinations: cotton and rayon, wool and orlon, or silk and nylon.
4. Observe and record your observations each week for three months. Which fabric began to deteriorate first? The fastest? Last? Slowest?
5. After three months, collect all the samples and examine under a stereoscope and a compound microscope. How do the synthetic fibers compare to the natural fibers? Are the natural or the synthetic fabrics more durable? What are some of the other factors that may have influenced your results?

Activity 3: DETECTING THE PRESENCE OF OZONE

MATERIALS (per student)

empty coffee cans
rubber bands
can opener (Church key type)
ultraviolet lamp
large heavy cardboard box or wooden box

METHODS

1. Construct Ozone Detectors. At the open end of an empty coffee can, make two holes on opposite sides with a can opener.
2. Stretch a rubber band across the opening and attach on the ends of the turned up metal.
3. Secure the rubber band by bending the metal over it. (Figure 4-7.)

Figure 4-7.

4. Place the ozone detectors in various areas around the school, community and home. Be certain to place some near electric motors because the electric charges produce ozone.
5. Check your ozone detectors each day and look for cracking and deterioration of the rubber. Record your observations. Where do you find most evidence for the presence of O_3?
6. As a standard of reference, set up a chamber with an ozone detector in it and an ultraviolet lamp (sun lamp). The chamber can be a large cardboard or wooden box. If there is a fume hood available, use it instead of the box. Face the lamp away from the window so it won't shine in anyone's eyes. U.V. radiation can damage the retina.
7. Shine the U.V. lamp on the rubber band. Check it each day and record your observations. Is deterioration inversely proportional to or directly proportional to the amount of U.V.

exposure? How does your controlled sample compare to the samples you tested in the field?

SOME NEW, PRACTICAL WAYS IN WHICH INDIVIDUALS CAN ASSIST EFFORTS TO CONTROL AIR POLLUTION

If everyone did his part, air pollution could be greatly reduced. Here are some ways we can all help.

1. Have the automobiles in your family checked by a mechanic. They may need tune-ups if they are producing too much carbon monoxide and unburned hydrocarbons. New plugs and points further reduce the amount of pollution emitted.
2. Keep an open mind regarding the purchase of new cars that do not have internal combustion engines. The new types pollute much less than the old design.
3. Avoid quick starts and stops in your motor vehicle. These actions can wear the rubber off the tires, asbestos off the brakes and asphalt off the road and thus add to air pollution to say nothing of the wear and tear on the car itself.
4. If you go somewhere, try to go on a public conveyance. If you must go by car, try to organize a car pool so that there will be more than two people per auto.
5. Use no-lead or low-lead gasolines in your motor vehicles. Try to convince others that low leaded gasolines pollute the air less than high leaded fuels.
6. Have the furnace in your house tested to see if it is burning efficiently. Call your fuel dealer and ask him about it. It will cost you less in the long run.
7. Use an electric, battery-powered or hand operated lawn mower rather than one propelled by gasoline and oil.
8. Keep outdoor burning to a minimum. Don't burn leaves or rubbish. Compost your leaves and other yard refuse. Some people even grind up their biodegradable (able to break down and decay) garbage and add it to their garden as fertilizer.
9. Don't smoke. It not only pollutes the air, it is also directly related to your own health.
10. Report polluters to the authorities and work for legislation that will clean up the air we breathe.

KEY POINTS

Key Points and Activities

Here is a checklist to help individuals control air pollution:

_____1. Auto tuned.

_____2. Auto has anti-pollution engine.

_____3. Auto operated properly—no fast starts and stops.

_____4. Use public transportation or ride in a car pool.

_____5. Use no-lead or low-lead gas.

_____6. Furnace efficient.

_____7. Lawn mower—not gas operated.

_____8. Compost leaves and biodegradable refuse.

_____9. Do not smoke.

_____10. Report polluters and work for cleaner air.

You may wish to reproduce the above list and distribute to your students, send to the P.T.A., and to the local newspaper to be printed as a public service.

GLOSSARY

aerosol — a suspension of insoluble particles in a gas.

greenhouse effect — the phenomenon in which energy in the form of light waves from the sun passes through the atmosphere and is absorbed by the earth. The earth then radiates this energy as heat waves which the air is able to absorb. Thus, it is said that the atmosphere acts similar to the glass of a greenhouse which allows in light waves and traps the heat.

liter — a unit for measuring volume; is equivalent to 1000 milliliters or 1000 cubic centimeters ($1 \text{ ml} = 1 \text{ cm}^3$).

ozone — (O_3)—a pungent, colorless, toxic gas which is formed when a single atom of oxygen combines with oxygen gas (O_2). It is one of the components of photochemical smog.

parts per million — (ppm)—a volume unit of measurement; the number of parts of a given pollutant in a million parts of something such as air, water, etc..

photochemical smog — a haze resulting from the chemical reactions and interactions of the pollutants in the air and light energy from the sun.

photosynthesis — the process by which certain living plant cells combine carbon dioxide and water in the presence of chlorophyll and light energy, to form carbohydrates for cell nourishment and release oxygen as a waste product.

Ringelmann Smoke Density Chart — a series of charts, numbered from 0—5, for measuring the density of black smoke arising from stacks and other sources (5 being most dense; and 0 least dense).

BIBLIOGRAPHY

Cailliet, Greg M., Paulette Y. Setzey, and Milton S. Love. *Everyman's Guide to Ecological Living.* New York: The Macmillan Company, 1971.

Congressional Quarterly. *Man's Control of the Environment.* 1735 K Street N.W. Washington, D.C.; Aug 1970.

Connecticut Department of Education: *Pollution: Problems, Projects, and Mathematical Exercises,* 1970.

Laun, H. Charles. *The Natural History Guide,* Alton, Illinois: Alsace Books & Films, 1970.

Lavaroni, Charles W., and Patrick A. O'Donnell. *Air Pollution.* Reading, Mass.: Addison-Wesley Publication, Inc., 1971.

Storin, Diane. *Investigating Air, Land, and Water Pollution.* Bronxville, N.Y.: Pawnee Publishing Company, Inc. 1971.

5

Water—Our Most Vital Resource

DISCOVERING THE UNIQUE PROPERTIES OF WATER

BACKGROUND

Water is one of the most amazing substances on earth and because it is so common, we often take it for granted. At ordinary temperatures, water is a clear, colorless liquid. Pure water (distilled or deionized) is flat and tasteless. The impurities in tap water give it a taste. In some areas, water is said to be *hard* because it contains salts of calcium and magnesium in the form of chlorides, carbonates, bicarbonates and sulfates. *Soft* water lacks these metallic salts. Pure water boils at 100 degrees Celsius and freezes at 0 degrees Celsius.

Water is called a *universal solvent* because more things dissolve in water than in anything else. This is an important factor in land erosion and in soil run off. Water dissolves the minerals in the soil and carries them to the streams, rivers and oceans. Fertilizer, which contains phosphates and nitrates, is washed into the lakes and streams and contributes to eutrophication.

Have your students ever wondered why the water in a pond freezes from the top down and not from the bottom up or why an ice cube floats in a glass of water? Most substances contract or shrink in size when they freeze but water expands. During the freezing process, water reaches its greatest density at 4 degrees Celsius. Thereafter, it begins to expand until it freezes at 0 degrees Celsius. Water is a polar covalent molecule, as shown in Figure 5-1.

Since the hydrogen part of the molecule is somewhat positive and the oxygen atoms are partially negative, the hydrogen of one molecule

$$\overset{+}{H} \quad 104.5° \quad \overset{+}{H}$$

$$\overset{\frown}{O}_{=}$$

Figure 5-1. Water Molecule

attracts the negative pole of another molecule. This attraction, attributed to the hydrogen bond effect, is responsible for the force that holds water molecules together. When water freezes, the molecules rearrange in a tetrahedron of hydrogen bonds around a water molecule, thus the water molecules are spaced farther apart. Look at the diagram of ice. (Figure 5-2.)

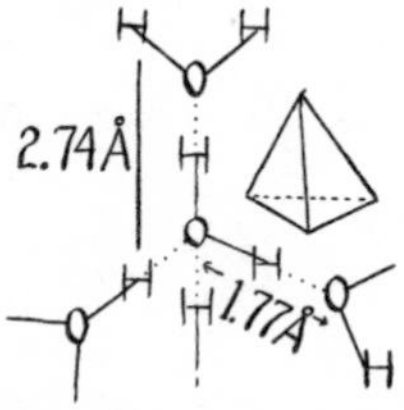

Figure 5-2. Ice

Water has many other unique properties. When objects are put in water they become wet. Why do water softeners make water "wetter"? When water falls, it forms drops. The surface of the water in a glass or graduated cylinder curves up along the sides of the glass. This is related to the hydrogen bond effect which exerts a force that holds the molecules of water together and is called *cohesion. Adhesion* is the force that is exerted *between* different substances such as the water and the glass. When we pour the water from the glass, the glass stays wet indicating that the force between the water and the glass is stronger than the cohesive forces. Water softeners break down the tension on the surface of water.

Activity 1: TASTING WATER

MATERIALS (per class)

    rain water
    plastic pan
    household iron filter

paper cups—2 per student
2 pitchers

METHODS

1. Collect some rain water in a clean, well rinsed plastic pan or demineralize (deionize) tap water with a household iron filter. (Figure 5-3.)

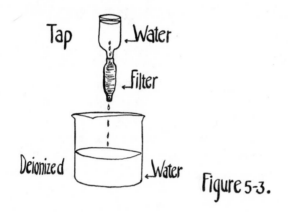

Tap .Water

.Filter

Deionized .Water

Figure 5-3.

2. Pour the pure water into a pitcher and label it "A." (Figure 5-4.)

A

Figure 5-4.

3. Run some tap water into a second pitcher and label it "B." (Figure 5-5.)

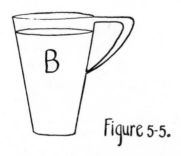

B

Figure 5-5.

4. Obtain two paper cups and label one cup "A" and the other cup "B." (Figure 5-6.)

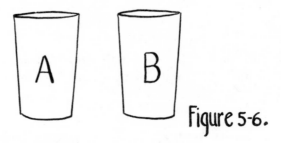

Figure 5-6.

5. Pour the water from the pitchers into the cups. "A" into "A," "B" into "B."
6. Taste the water in cup "A" first and describe the taste.
7. Taste the water in cup "B" and write down a description of the taste.

Do you have an idea why tap water has a taste? Besides the metallic salts mentioned above, tap water has chlorine in it to retard bacterial growth and in some places, fluorine has been added to prevent tooth decay.

Activity 2:   DETECTING CALCIUM AND MAGNESIUM SALTS IN THE WATER

MATERIALS (per class)

1 pint glass jar
   test tubes
   Calcium Hydroxide [$Ca(OH)_2$]
   Sodium Carbonate (Na_2CO_3)

METHODS

1. Make up a stock solution of calcium hydroxide. Cover the bottom of a pint jar with calcium hydroxide and fill the jar with distilled (deionized or rain) water. Stir with a glass rod.
2. Deliver approximately 1 cm^3 of $Ca(OH)_2$ into a test tube containing tap water and 1 cm^3 into another test tube containing rain water.
3. Stir with a wooden splint or glass rod. Record your observations. The calcium hydroxide combines with the calcium hydrogen carbonate to form an insoluble, solid white precipitate, calcium carbonate, and water:

$$Ca(HCO_3)_2 \quad + \quad Ca(OH)_2 \longrightarrow 2CaCO_3 \quad + 2H_2O$$

Ca(HCO₃)₂	+	Ca(OH)₂		2CaCO₃	+ 2H₂O
calcium hydrogen carbonate	+	calcium hydroxide	yields	calcium carbonate (precipitate)	water

Calcium hydroxide also combines with magnesium hydrogen carbonate and magnesium chloride to form insoluble magnesium hydroxide and calcium carbonate. If magnesium chloride is present, calcium chloride is also formed:

Mg(HCO₃)₂	+	Ca(OH)₂	
magnesium hydrogen carbonate	+	calcium hydroxide	yields

Mg(OH)₂ ↓	+	CaCO₃ ↓	+ H₂O	+ CO₂ ↑
magnesium hydroxide (precipitate)	+	calcium carbonate (precipitate)	+water	+ carbon dioxide

MgCl₂	+	Ca(OH)₂		Mg(OH)₂ ↓	+ CaCl₂ ↓
magnesium chloride	+	calcium hydroxide	yields	magnesium hydroxide (precipitate)	+ calcium chloride (precipitate)

Hold the test tubes to the light to see the formation of the precipitates.

4. Let the test tubes stand until all the solid compounds have settled. To remove additional calcium ions, add washing soda (sodium carbonate).

CaCl₂	+	Na₂CO₃		CaCO₃ ↓	+	2NaCl
calcium chloride	+	sodium carbonate	yields	calcium carbonate (precipitate)	+	sodium chloride

CaSO₄		Na₂CO₃		CaCO₃ ↓	+	Na₂SO₄
calcium sulfate	+	sodium carbonate	yields	calcium carbonate (precipitate)	+	sodium sulfate

Activity 3:   EXPERIMENTING WITH SOLVENTS AND SOLUTES

MATERIALS (per student)

18 250 ml beakers	citric acid
water	moth flakes
alcohol	magnesium
benzene	magnesium carbonate
sugar	cooking oil

METHODS

1. A *solute* is the substance that dissolves and the *solvent* does the dissolving. Prepare eighteen 250 ml beakers with three different solvents. Pour water, alcohol (denatured ethanol, methanol, or isopropyl alcohol) and benzene (cleaning fluid) into each of six beakers. Fill only 1/2 inch high.

2. Label the water beakers W1, W2, and so on. Label the alcohol beakers A1, A2, etc. and the benzene beakers B1, B2....(Figure 5-7.)

Figure 5-7.

3. Add a teaspoon of sugar to beakers numbered 1. Stir with a glass rod or a wooden splint. Record observations on a chart according to the degree of solubility of each solute in each solvent—insoluble, slightly soluble, soluble, very soluble. (Chart No. 3)

Chart No. 3

Substance	Solubility in water	Solubility in alcohol	Solubility in benzene
1. Sugar	VS	SS	
2. Citric Acid	VS	VS	
3. Moth Flakes	I	S	
4. Magnesium	I	I	
5. Magnesium carbonate	I	I	
6. Cooking oil			

Activity 4: INVESTIGATING WHAT HAPPENS TO WATER WHEN IT FREEZES

MATERIALS (per student)

medicine vial or small plastic container
magic marker or grease pen

METHODS

1. Obtain a plastic medicine vial or some other small plastic container and fill it 3/4 full of water.
2. Mark the water level on the container with a magic marker or a grease pencil so you will know how much water has been added. (Figure 5-8.)

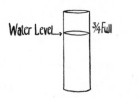

Figure 5-8.

3. Place the container in the freezer.
4. When the water has frozen solid, remove it from the freezer and examine it. Does the amount of ice seem to be greater, lesser or equal to the amount of water originally put in the container? Does water exist in any other phase than in the liquid and solid phases? Does the molecular structure of water or the arrangement of molecules change as water changes from one phase to another?
5. Place ice cubes in water. What happens? What do your observations tell you about the density of ice and water? What is density?

Activity 5:   TESTING THE COHESIVENESS OF WATER

MATERIALS (per student)

plate glass 3" x 5"
balance
shallow dish
water

METHODS

1. Obtain a piece of plate glass about 3" x 5" in size. Weigh it on a balance and record the weight.
2. Tie the plate of glass to the balance beam and lower it into a shallow dish of water.

3. Add weights to the other balance pan until the cohesive force holding the glass to the surface of the water breaks. Did this take more force than represented by the weight of the glass, less force or an equal force? What can you conclude about the strength of the hydrogen bonds that hold the water molecules together?

HOW TO FIND THE DENSITY OF WATER

BACKGROUND

Density is a characteristic property which helps us distinguish substances from each other. If we were to take many samples of water from a gallon or liter of water, we would find that each sample would have the same mass. The mass of a given volume is a characteristic property of a substance and is useful in distinguishing between various substances. Density is the mass of one unit volume of a substance and is expressed usually as grams/cubic centimeter (g/cm^3).

We can find the density of a sample of any quantity of substance by measuring the mass, measuring the volume and then dividing the mass by the volume to obtain the mass per unit of volume.

$$\text{Density} = \frac{\text{mass}}{\text{volume}}, \quad D = \frac{M}{V}$$

Activity 1:   TO DETERMINE THE DENSITY OF WATER

MATERIALS (per student)

balance
graduated cylinder
small beaker or measuring cup
water

METHODS

1. In the graduated cylinder, measure 10 cm^3 of water. This is the volume.
2. Find the mass of an empty beaker or measuring cup by using the balance.
3. Pour the 10 cm^3 of water into the beaker.

4. Find the mass of the beaker plus the water.
5. Now calculate the mass of the water alone.
6. Remembering that density is determined by dividing the mass by the volume, find the density of 1 cm^3 of water (D $= \dfrac{M}{V}$).
7. Record your results as follows:

Mass of beaker + water _____
Mass of beaker alone _____
Mass of water alone _____
Density of 1 cm^3 water _____

DETERMINING THE TURBIDITY, ODOR AND COLOR OF WATER

BACKGROUND

Turbidity is the opposite of transparency and refers to the amount of material suspended in the water. When you shine a beam of light into water, it is reflected, refracted, absorbed, scattered or transmitted depending upon the quantity of suspended matter in the water.

Turbidity affects the depth to which light can penetrate and thereby has an affect on the photosynthetic activity of a body of water.

The degree of turbidity in water is measured with the use of a secchi disc and color standards.

Water color is due partially to the amount and color of materials suspended in the water. Water color can be seen by holding a sample of water in a clear glass tube against a white background.

Normally water is odorless. The presence of odors is thus dependent upon the existence of plankton and chemical and organic wastes. Few odors should be detected from a normal healthy body of water. Odors often occur when the dissolved oxygen (DO) content is too low for aerobic (with air present) respiration to take place. Anaerobic (without air) bacteria decompose the organic matter and produce methane gas (CH_4)—also called *marsh gas*—and active hydrogen. The anaerobic bacteria also use the oxygen that is bound in NO_3 (nitrite), SO_3 (sulfite) or SO_4 (sulfate) ions. Ammonia gas (NH_3) and hydrogen sulfide (H_2S) are formed. Odors of these gases—methane, ammonia and hydrogen sulfide—are an indication that the DO concentration is low.

Give your students some experience in water analysis as suggested below.

Activity 1:   TO EXAMINE THE TURBIDITY OF WATER

MATERIALS (per team of 2 or 3 students)

1—Secchi disc—this may be purchased or homemade.
Homemade procedures:
1. Cut an 8" diameter disc from aluminum or heavy sheet metal—
paint black and white. (Figure 5-9.)

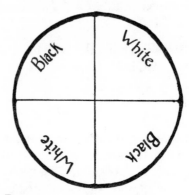

Figure 5-9. Secchi Disc

OR,
2. Use the white top of a gallon jar 4"-5" in diameter. Screw a
metal weight to the bottom so it will sink. (Figure 5-10.)

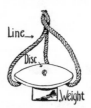

Figure 5-10. Secchi Disc

3. Tie on 15 feet of line (rope) with markings or tie knots every one
foot, or 30.5 cm.

METHOD

1. Slowly lower disc into water. Be sure to keep the line vertical.
2. Continue to lower disc until it can no longer be seen. Record this
depth. _____
3. Allow disc to sink a few more feet.

4. Pull disc up until it becomes visible again. Record this depth.
5. Average the two depths for the final reading. _____._____
6. Compare various sections of the body of water, also compare the turbidity of different bodies of water.

Activity 2: TO PERFORM A COLOR ANALYSIS WITH THE FOREL AND ULE SCALES AND THE SECCHI DISC

MATERIALS (per team of 2 or 3 students)

Secchi disc with cord or chain
Forel Scale for deep waters
Ule Scale for shallow waters

METHODS

1. Lower the Secchi disc one meter into the water.
2. Hold the Forel or Ule scale at the top of the water over the Secchi disc.
3. Compare the color of the water on the Secchi disc with the vials in the scales.
4. Record the color. ____._____
5. Compare colors at various depths and locations.

Activity 3: TO DETECT AND IDENTIFY ODOR IN A WATER SAMPLE

MATERIALS (per student)

water sample bottle
long cord

METHOD

1. You can construct your own water sample bottle. (Figure 5-11.)
2. Allow container to sink to desired depth. Be sure cord is vertical.
3. Pull cord to free stopper.
4. Allow water to enter container.
5. Record the depth from which sample was taken. _____
6. Raise container and collect contents.
7. Inhale cautiously and record the odors detected.
8. Collect samples from various depths and locations.

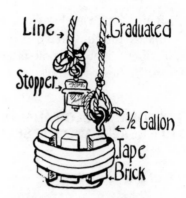

Figure 5-11. Sampling Bottle

MEASURING THE pH OF WATER

BACKGROUND

Briefly, *pH* refers to the concentration of positive hydrogen ions and negative hydroxyl ions in water. Water with a pH of 7.0 has equivalent hydrogen (H^+) and hydroxyl ions (OH^-) and is neutral. A pH of less than 7.0 shows an increase of hydrogen ions and is acidic. A pH above 7.0 has a higher concentration of hydroxyl ions and is alkaline or basic. Most fresh water lakes have a pH range between 6.5—8.5. Extremes in pH above and below this range usually indicate the presence of pollutants.

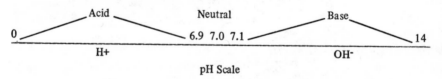

Activity 1:   TO ESTIMATE THE pH OF WATER

MATERIALS (per student)

litmus paper
hydrion paper
5 clean glass jars
forceps

METHODS

1. Collect samples of water in a clean, well rinsed jar.

2. Select several locations for sampling and take at least 5 samples and label the jars.

3. Using forceps, dip a piece of red litmus paper into each of the five jars. Use a different piece of litmus paper for each jar. Record your observations.

   Red litmus turns blue in base.
   Red litmus remains red in acid.
   Red litmus remains red if solution is neutral.

4. Repeat the procedures in number 3 above using Blue Litmus paper.

   Blue litmus turns red in acid.
   Blue litmus remains blue in base.
   Blue litmus remains blue if solution is neutral.

5. Discard the neutral water samples and continue to test with hydrion paper. Hydrion paper is more specific and will give a more accurate pH reading between 1 and 14. Dip the hydrion paper into the water sample and compare the color change, if any, with the standard on the chart attached to the container.

CALCULATING THE RATE AND DIRECTION OF FLOW IN A RIVER OR STREAM

BACKGROUND

Nearly 40% of all the water that falls on the earth flows back to the sea either as surface water or in underground streams. The surface water of our rivers and streams is called *runoff,* or *running water.*

Several factors affecting the velocity of the runoff include the amount and type of rainfall, the slope or gradient of the area receiving the rainfall, the type of material over which the water flows and the amount and kind of vegetation present.

Runoff is rapid on steep slopes carrying with it loose particles of rock and soil until the river has eventually eroded downward to form rills. As the gradient of the stream bed becomes lower, the rills are widened to gullies and eventually to ravines.

Maturity of a river is reached when the slope of the riverbed has been reduced until the velocity is just enough to carry the load. At this time the river channel is well established. Downward erosion is nearly complete and the stream now begins cutting sidewards and widening its valley. As the water travels sideward, it develops S-shaped curves which are called *meanders.* A meandering stream continues to erode on the outside of the curves where the velocity is greater and deposits silt on the inside of the curves where the velocity is reduced. Thus, even though a river has been slowed down by old age, it continues to change in appearance.

Some suggested activities for your students to do follow.

Activity 1:   DETERMINING THE RATE AND DIRECTION OF FLOW IN A RIVER

MATERIALS (per class)

flowing water—may be a river or the water pouring out of a drain
             pipe in the school yard or the gutter at the curb.
small white cards
markers
watch with sweep second hand

METHODS

1. Place markers at two different points on your river.
2. Drop one or two small white cards into the water at the upper marker.
3. Observe the cards as they float from the upper marker to the lower one.
4. Record your observations of the river and the card and the time it took for the card to float between the markers.
5. Repeat at different locations, at different times of day and at different seasons.

Additional activities and observations that can be made of your school yard river:

1. Trace the river's path and look for features that may be found in large rivers.
2. Is your river carrying any material away with it? If so, what is the source of this material?
3. Collect a glass of the river water. Observe and record its appearance and odor. Cover it and set it aside for later observations. Has anything settled out of the water in your glass? Record your observations.
4. Build a dam with debris found in the river. As the water rises behind the dam, what happens to the materials carried in your river? Do you think this would be a problem behind the big dams on our rivers and lakes? Try to think of some alternatives and solutions.

5. Where does the water from your tiny school yard river eventually go?

FINDING THE AMOUNT OF OXYGEN IN WATER

BACKGROUND

Without oxygen, most organisms cannot live. Aquatic life makes use of the oxygen dissolved in the water. Therefore, dissolved oxygen (DO) content can be used as an index of water quality.

A simple method for determing the amount of DO in water is the Methylene Blue Procedure. In oxygen rich water, methylene blue retains its dark blue color. In oxygen poor water, methylene blue fades until the solution is clear, indicating that little or no oxygen is present.

Activity 1:   FINDING THE AMOUNT OF OXYGEN IN WATER

MATERIALS (per class)

Methylene Blue indicator solution
test tubes
water-collecting bottles
watch with sweep second hand or timer
stoppered medicine vials

METHOD: Methylene Blue Procedure

1. Pour 10 ml of sample water in a test tube.
2. Add 2 ml of Methylene Blue to sample water.
3. Record the amount of time it takes for the color to change from dark blue to light or clear.
4. Repeat the procedure for the same water supply.
5. Repeat the procedure for other water samples and compare.

INTERPRETATION

The faster the color change takes place, the less oxygen is present, the more carbon dioxide is probably in the sample, and the more bacteria are in the water. Make up a set of Standards (use medicine vials) from +1 to +4 indicating the concentration of DO in the water. Let +1 be the oxygen poor concentration and +4 the oxygen rich concentration. In which samples do you find the oxygen rich water, that is, from which source or sources do your oxygen rich samples come? Would you expect to find a high DO concentration in the rapids of a stream or a low DO concentration? Try to explain your reasoning.

WAYS TO GET ACTION FOR BETTER WATER USAGE

Most states now have clean water legislation that stipulates that no one has the right to pollute our waterways. We know, however, that sometimes laws are not enforced.

The first thing for an individual or group to do is to gather data on the way water resources are actually being used or abused. If you and your class suspect that a local river is being contaminated by sewage from homes or industry or that industry is dumping chemical wastes into the water, set up a vigilance schedule. Look for open drains and runoff areas. Take photographs of suspected sources of pollution and record the date and time of each observation.

Follow through by having your students conduct some of the tests described in this handbook, record, and document their findings.

Urge them to go to the local library and the town hall and inquire as to what legislation has been passed on water usage. Suggest that they read these documents to determine if someone may be violating the laws.

Have a team of two or three students make an appointment to present their case to your local Conservation Commission and enlist their aid. If they do not get the cooperation of the local agency, have them go directly to the state agency, the Department of Environmental Protection, and phone their State Representatives.

If you and your class still do not get action, write to the Environmental Protection, Agency of the Federal Government in Washington, D.C. and contact your Senators and Congressmen. Meanwhile, have some students consult the Chamber of Commerce or town hall and obtain a list of all the agencies in your town and contact those organizations that might be interested in protecting our waterways. Such organizations as the League of Women Voters, the American Association of University Women, the Garden Clubs, the Junior Womens Club, the Girl Scouts and Boy Scouts are usually willing to assist in a good cause.

KEY POINTS

Key Points and Activities

No one has the right to pollute our water resources.
Ways to get action—

1. Observe and gather data.
2. Test, record and prepare brief statements.
3. Check legislation, present laws and regulations in town hall and library.
4. Go to local Conservation Commission.
5. Contact the state Department of Environmental Protection.
6. Phone your State Representatives.
7. Write to the U.S. Environmental Protection Agency.
8. Contact your Senators and Congressmen.
9. Obtain a list of local agencies from the Chamber of Commerce or town hall.
10. Contact organizations to render assistance.

GLOSSARY

adhesion — the force exerted between different substances.

anaerobic — refers to organisms which grow only in the absence of air (oxygen).

cohesion — the force that holds like molecules together.

hard water — water which contains salts of calcium and magnesium in the form of chlorides, carbonates, bicarbonates and sulfates.

pH — refers to the concentration of positive hydrogen ions and negative hydroxyl ions in water. Water with a pH of 7.0 has equivalent hydrogen (H^+) and hydroxyl (OH^-) ions and is neutral.

polar covalent molecule — a molecule in which the slightly less than equal sharing of electrons in the bonding results in a small positive and negative residual charge at each end of the molecule.

precipitate — the solid produced by the chemical combination of different compounds or elements. It settles out of solution.

pure water — HOH or H_2O. It is clean rain water, distilled or deionized— in other words, free from impurities.

soft water — lacks the metallic salts present in hard water.

solute — a substance that dissolves when mixed with something else (the solvent).

solvent — a substance that does the dissolving when mixed with something else (the solute).

BIBLIOGRAPHY

Ahrens, Maurice R., Norris F. Bush and Ray K. Easley. *Living Chemistry*. Boston: Ginn and Company, 1961.

Blaustein, Elliot H. *Anti-pollution Lab*. N.Y.: Sentinel Books Publishers Inc., 1972.

Dull, Charles E., H. Clark Metcalfe and John E. Williams. *Modern Chemistry*. N.Y.: Holt Rinehart and Winston, Inc., 1962.

Garrett, Alfred B., John S. Richardson and Earl J. Montague. *Chemistry—A First Course in Modern Chemistry*. Boston: Ginn and Co., 1966.

Investigating the Earth. Earth Science Curriculum Project (ESCP). Boston: Houghton Mifflin Co., 1967.

Laun, H. Charles. *The National History Guide*. Alton, Ill.: Alsace Books and Films, 1970.

Lemkin, William. *Visualized General Science*. N.Y.: Oxford Book Co., 1964.

Rabinowitz, Alan, Toby Bates Sutton and Edward M. Taylor. *Oceanography: An Environmental Approach to Marine Science*. Hoboken, N.J.: Oceanography Unlimited, 1970.

Storin, Diane. *Investigating Air, Land and Water Pollution*. N.Y.: Pawnee Publishing Co., Inc., 1971.

6

Examining Water Pollutants

LOOKING FOR EVIDENCE OF FECAL CONTAMINATION

BACKGROUND

Increased population with its accompanying increases in homes has brought with it a problem of water contamination due to sewage disposal. Human excreta contains both pathogenic and non-pathogenic bacteria which can enter our water supply through the discharge effluent from sewage treatment plants or by leaching through the soil where private wells and septic systems are used.

A species of nonpathogenic bacteria which normally inhabit, in a commensal relationship, the large intestines of man and other animals is called a *coliform*. The most common occurring species (80 - 95% of all coliforms) in man is *Escherichia coli* (*E. coli*). Thus, the presence of *E. coli* in water is an indication of contamination by fecal matter and the probable presence of pathogens. Pathogenic (disease producing) organisms usually do not survive once they leave the host and therefore, the Public Health Service has established standards for coliform levels as an indication of the acceptability of the water for drinking, swimming, or other uses.

Activity 1:   A SIMPLE TEST FOR DETECTING BACTERIA IN WATER

MATERIALS (per team of 2 or 3 students)

 pint or .473 liters water-collecting bottle with screw top
6 plastic coffee can covers or 3 Petri dishes

box of plain gelatin and boullion cubes or E.M.B. agar
plastic tape
felt tip marking pen or grease pencil
medicine dropper
toothpicks or inoculating loops

METHODS

1. Wash your hands with soap and water. Mix up gelatin as directed on the box and add one boullion cube. Heat and pour into three plastic covers or Petri dishes. Cover them with another plastic top and let set. Prepare and use E.M.B. agar as directed on the label.
2. Prepare your water collecting bottles by washing them thoroughly and rinsing at least ten times. Do the same with the medicine dropper.
3. Collect your water sample from a pond, well, stream or elsewhere and screw on the top securely. Use immediately or store in the refrigerator or in a cool place out of direct light.
4. When ready to use your water sample, shake the bottle in a standard method, that is, seven times in the space of one foot or 30.5 cm; in an arc of 90 degrees in seven seconds. This is done in order to distribute the organisms uniformly.
5. Wash your hands to avoid contamination, and open one plastic covered plate to expose the gelatin. Quickly pour in 1 ml of water from your sample bottle. Rotate it to cover evenly. Replace the cover and tape it closed. Label it "1 ml water" and mark the date.
6. Take your clean medicine dropper and fill it one half full of your water sample. Deliver this amount on the side of a second gelatin plate. Streak the water over the gelatin with a clean toothpick or inoculating loop. Cover and seal it with tape. Label it "1/2 medicine dropper" and mark the date.
7. Leave the third gelatin plate as is without adding water. Tape it closed and label it "Control" and mark the date.
8. Incubate the three cultures in an incubator at 37 degrees Celsius for 24 hours, or in a warm, dark place at room temperature for 48 hours.
9. Examine your cultures after 24 and 48 hours. There should be evidence of growth on the agar or gelatin of the plates inoculated with the questionable water. The control plate should not have growth on it.
10. Examine the growth with a strong magnifying glass or under a

stereoscope. Describe. Do all the colonies look alike? Could there be more than one organism growing in the culture?
11. Soak plates in Lysol overnight and then discard.

Activity 2:   A MODIFIED AMERICAN PUBLIC HEALTH ASSOCIATION (A.P.H.A.) TEST FOR COLIFORM BACTERIA

MATERIALS (per team or 2 or 3 students)

Presumptive Test sets (5 Durham fermentation tubes containing Lactose Broth)
Confirmative Test sets (5 Durham fermentation tubes containing Brilliant Green Lactose Bile Broth)
Test sets can be obtained from:

Hach Chemical Company
Box 907
Ames, Iowa 50010

Oceanography Unlimited, Inc.
1000 Clinton Street
Hoboken, N.J.

METHODS

1. Wash your hands thoroughly with soap and water to avoid contaminating the test vials.
2. Remove a vial from the *Presumptive Test* set.
3. Carefully, unscrew the top. Do not touch the inside of the cap or vial.
4. Fill the vial with the sample water to be tested. Screw on the top securely.
5. Invert the vial until the small tube inside is free of bubbles.
6. Repeat above with remaining 4 vials.
7. Incubate the 5 vials in an incubator at $37^{\circ}C$ for 24 hours or in a warm place for 48 hours.
8. After 1/2 hour, check the vials again for bubbles. Invert those which have bubbles in the inner tube to expel the air. Continue to incubate.
9. Check tubes after 12 to 24 hours. If gas collects in the inner tube, coliform bacteria are assumed to be present. If no gas collects, incubate up to 48 hours.
10. If after 48 hours, no gas has collected, coliform bacteria are assumed to be absent from the test water sample.

INTERPRETATION

Presence of gas in Lactose Broth *may* mean the presence of coliforms but it is not positive. Other bacteria may produce gas, and therefore, it is necessary to test further and to inoculate Brilliant Green Lactose Bile Broth.

11. Remove the vials from the *Confirmative Test* set.
12. Invert the *Presumptive Test* vials showing gas in the inner tube. This insures that some bacteria are on the screw top cap.
13. Carefully, transfer a wet screw top cap from the *Presumptive Test* vial to one of the *Confirmative Test* vials.
14. Repeat until all caps have been transferred from the positive Presumptive vials to the Confirmative vials.
15. Incubate as above.

INTERPRETATION

Presence of gas in the *Confirmative Test* vials confirms the presence of coliform organisms in the test water. The presence of coliform bacteria indicates the sample water was contaminated with fecal material which may or may not also harbor pathogenic (disease causing) organisms like typhoid, paratyphoid, dysentery, etc.

The number of coliform bacteria per 100 ml. of water can be estimated by the number of tubes containing gas as follows:

No. of tubes containing gas	*No. Coliforms/100 ml*
0	none
1	2.2*
2	5.1
3	9.2
4	16
5	over 16

Activity 3:   USING THE MEMBRANE FILTRATION METHOD OF DETECTING COLIFORM ORGANISMS IN WATER

MATERIALS (per team of 2 or 3 students)

Millipore Sterifil apparatus with type HAWG filter
Millipore Swinnex - 25 Holder with type GS filter
Petri dish and pad with MF - Endo Medium (pink)

---

*Less than 2.2 coliforms/100 ml is the acceptable amount for drinking water according to the 1962 U.S. Public Health Drinking Water Standards.

syringe
ml pipette
pair forceps
hand lens or stereoscope
Bunsen burner or alcohol lamp
some sterile distilled water

METHOD

1. Fill a syringe with 10 ml sterile distilled water.
2. Filter the sterile distilled water through a Swinnex - 25 into a Sterifil funnel.
3. Pipette 2/10 ml (4 drops) of test water into the Sterifil funnel & swirl to mix it with the dilution water.
4. Filter the diluted sample.
5. Flame a forceps and remove the filter and place it on the pad in the Petri dish with medium. Replace the cover on the Petri dish.
6. Incubate the Petri dish for 24 hours at $37^{\circ}C$ or for 48 hours in a dark place at room temperature.
7. After the incubation period, remove the filter with flamed forceps and place on a clean paper towel to dry.
8. Examine the filter with a hand lens or under a stereoscope. Look for colonies of bacteria having a shiny greenish surface. Count them. This is the number of coliforms present in the 2/10 ml sample (4 drops) of water tested. How many organisms would be present in 1 gallon of water? (Multiply by 22,730.)

Activity 4:   ENDO AGAR CONFIRMED TEST FOR COLIFORMS

MATERIALS (per team of 2 or 3 students)

tube positive (presumptive test showed probable presence of coliforms) lactose broth culture
2 Petri dishes with Endo agar
bacteriological loop
Bunsen burner or alcohol lamp

METHOD

1. Flame bacteriological loop, remove cotton stopper or screw top from lactose broth culture and flamp top of vial or tube.
2. Insert loop and remove loopful of culture.

3. Flame vial or tube and quickly replace stopper so as not to contaminate culture.
4. Carefully remove bottom of Petri dish and streak Endo agar. Return to cover.
5. Incubate Endo agar culture for 24 hours at $37^{\circ}C$ or for 48 hours at room temperature. (Place them upside down to prevent moisture from collecting on the surface of agar.)
6. After the incubation period, examine the colonies with a hand lens or under a stereoscope. Typical colonies of *Escherichia coli* when grown on Endo Agar produce a characteristic reddening of the medium. They also precipitate the fuchsin dye on the top of the colonies giving them a metallic sheen.

ADDITIONAL OPTIONAL ACTIVITY

If you wish to look at the colonies under the oil immersion lens of your microscope, stain them using Gram's staining technique. They will then appear as short plump Gram negative (red) rods occurring singly, in pairs or in short chains. (Staining directions can be found in any elementary bacteriology book.)

TESTING FOR CHEMICAL POLLUTANTS

BACKGROUND

The chemicals present in our water supply are from two sources: (1) those naturally present such as carbonates which may come from the rock layers through which the water has passed; or, (2) sulfates, phosphates, nitrates and chlorine which are still present in the effluent that is discharged as treated from sewage treatment plants.

Approximately one third of the public sewage treatment plants in the United States are only primary treatment plants. These are designed to remove sticks, papers, sludge, and debris which can be trapped by screens. Secondary treatment, coupled with chlorination, effectively removes 90 percent of degradable organic waste and 99 percent of the "germs" in the water. Privately owned septic systems might be compared to secondary treatment plants without the chlorination feature.

Tertiary sewage treatment, which utilizes filtration, flocculation, and other mechanical and chemical processes, removes almost all of the contaminants from water. But tertiary treatment plants are terribly expensive to construct and maintain, consequently there are very few in existence. Phone or visit your local treatment plant, and ask the sanitary engineer which process they use to treat the sewage.

It should be easy to see how phosphates, nitrates, and sulfates from detergents, and chlorine from bleach, can find their way back into our water supply. Additionally, the runoff from surface water eventually carries the sulfates, nitrates, and phosphates from garden fertilizers as well as chemicals from pesticides and insecticides into our streams and rivers which ultimately become someone's domestic water supply.

The Federal Housing Authority (F.H.A.) requires that water be analyzed before approving loans on certain property. Water is tested for nitrates, detergents, chlorides, iron, manganese, hardners and pH. Iron is undesirable because of the damage it does to the fixtures and clothes. Manganese damages the pipes and stains the plumbing fixtures. Hardness refers to the degree water can form lather from soap.

Hard water usually contains the dissolved chemicals magnesium chloride ($MgCl_2$), magnesium sulfate ($MgSO_4$), calcium chloride ($CaCl_2$), and calcium sulfate ($CaSO_4$), or the bicarbonates of the metals. Soap will dissolve easily in soft water to form suds but no suds will form in hard water. The salts above react with the soap to form insoluble products which eventually settle (precipitate).

The pH is also important because if water is too acidic, it can damage plumbing equipment and pipes.

Activity 1:   TESTING FOR HARD WATER

MATERIALS (per team of 2 or 3 students)

> distilled or deionized water
> water sample to be tested
2 500 ml flasks
> pure soap (Ivory flakes, castille, etc.)

METHOD

1. Fill a 500 ml flask with distilled water. Add 1 tablespoon of soap. Shake and let stand a few minutes.
2. Fill a second 500 ml flask with water to be tested. Add 1 tablespoon of soap. Shake and let stand a few minutes.
3. Compare both flasks. What do you observe? Is your sample water hard or soft? To what degree might you describe its hardness?

Activity 2:   MEASURING THE pH OF POLLUTED WATER

MATERIALS (per team of 2 or 3 students)

red and blue litmus paper
hydrion paper
pH meter
forceps
400 ml beaker

METHODS

1. Using forceps, insert one strip of red litmus paper in your sample water. If it turns blue, the water is basic. If it remains the same color, the water can either be neutral or acidic.
2. Repeat No. 1. using Blue Litmus. If the blue litmus turns red, the water is acidic. If it remains blue, the water is either neutral or basic.
3. Record your results. Why is it necessary to use both Red and Blue Litmus together rather than using only one or the other?
4. Once you have determined that your sample water is acidic or basic, test with Hydrion paper and compare its color with the chart on the Hydrion paper container to get a more accurate pH reading. Record. _____
5. If a pH meter is available, lower the electrodes into a beaker of sample water. Turn the dial and record the exact pH of your sample. How acidic or basic is it?

Activity 3:   TITRATION METHOD FOR DETERMINING CARBON DIOXIDE IN WATER

MATERIALS (per team of 2 or 3 students)

44 N standard sodium hydroxide
0.5% phenolphthalein indicator
250 ml Erlenmeyer flask
25 ml Burette
Burette stand
Burette clamp

METHOD

1. Without agitating, pour 200 ml of water to be tested into the Erlenmeyer flask. Stopper immediately until ready to use.

2. Fill the Burette with the Standard NaOH for titration.
3. Remove stopper from the water and add 5 drops of phenolphthalein solution and begin to titrate the NaOH into the flask immediately one half to one drop at a time. Swirl the flask after each drop.
4. Stop immediately when the pink color remains in solution.
5. Record the amount of NaOH needed to neutralize the CO_2 dissolved in water. Multiply this number by 5 and you will have the amount of free CO_2 in the water in ppm. _____

Tests for some of the other chemicals mentioned in this chapter are complicated. However, many commercial companies have developed simplified methods of testing for the presence and concentrations of chemicals found in water. You might want to obtain kits so your students can run tests on chlorine and chloride, detergents, iron, manganese, and nitrates. You may wish to contact Hach, Oceanography Unlimited or LaMotte Chemical Companies regarding their kits.

LaMotte Chemical Products Co., Chestertown, Md. 21620
Hach Chemical Company, Box 907, Ames, Iowa 50010
Oceanography Unlimited Inc., 1000 Clinton St., Hoboken, N.J.

EVALUATING THERMAL EFFECTS ON WATER

BACKGROUND

The demand for more electric power continues to increase, presenting a dual problem. Without more power plants, the United States faces a critical electrical power shortage, but on the other hand, the more power plants we have, the more air and water pollution results. According to the environmentalists, electric power plants are among the worst polluters. Although the answer to the power shortage seems to be nuclear energy, atomic plants present a radiation hazard and heat up the water causing thermal effects. By changing the temperature of the water, the environment of the plants and animals living in the area is also changed.

The nuclear power plants use water in lakes and rivers to cool the reactor. The water never comes in contact with the radioactive core or nuclear fuel itself but just circulates in an outer protected jacket and absorbs heat. The water is then returned to the natural body of water at a higher temperature, sometimes up to and more than 23 degrees warmer than when it entered the power plant. The methods by which water is returned vary with the location of the nuclear power plants. Some use cooling towers, others long canals.

Research on what happens to the plants and animals living in an area where the water is warmed continues. Thus far, findings indicate that some effects are harmful and others are not. What can your students add to this information?

Activity 1:   THERMAL EFFECTS ON AN AQUARIUM

MATERIALS (per team of 2 or 3 students)

    aquarium and accessories
    water plants and animals
    thermometer
    aquarium heater

METHOD

1. Look up how to start fresh and salt water (marine) aquariums.
2. Decide on which one you want to set up and obtain the materials you need.
3. Look up the conditions necessary for your plants and animals to live well. Pay particular attention to the temperature range that is recommended.
4. After a week or two, your aquarium should be stabilized and you are ready to experiment.
5. Raise the temperature a few degrees every four days until you reach the lowest maximum temperature for survival of one organism in your tank.
6. Thereafter, raise the temperature only one degree more and record all your observations. Did the rise in temperature change the behavior of the organisms in your aquatic ecosystem? Did they remain healthy? Did they adjust to the temperature change?

Activity 2:   KEEPING TRACK OF TEMPERATURE CHANGES AT THE MOUTH OF A NUCLEAR POWER PLANT CANAL

(*Note:* If this activity is not possible, have students search the literature and review the research done on thermal effects.)

MATERIALS (per student or team of 2 or 3 students)

    indoor-outdoor thermometer

METHOD

1. At first, take the temperature of the air and water at different times during the day and week to determine the peak times for the highest temperatures.
2. Looking at your findings, set up a schedule and take the reading at the same times each day and the same days each week at the mouth of a nuclear power plant canal.
3. Record your findings and plot a graph of your results.
4. Return to the area and begin to study the plants and animals and see if their behavior changes as the temperature changes. Is the aquatic life different downstream than that found above the atomic power plant?

Activity 3: STUDYING OTHER FACTORS AFFECTING TEMPERATURE CHANGES IN WATER

MATERIALS (per student or team of 2 or 3 students)

6   pint jars exactly alike
6   laboratory thermometers
    various elements, detergent, bleach, manure, garbage, etc.

METHOD

1. Standardize the thermometers by placing them in the same jar of tap water undisturbed for at least 15 minutes. Select the thermometer with the highest reading and record the differences of each thermometer on a piece of masking tape and tape it on the thermometers. Add this number to your readings.
2. Place various materials in your jars such as mentioned above.
3. Fill each jar to the same level with tap water. Fill one jar with tap water only and label it "Control."
4. Place the jars in the sunlight or in a warm place. Let stabilize for 15 minutes and then begin to record the temperature of each jar.
5. Leave the thermometers in the jars and record the temperatures every 15 minutes until no more changes have taken place.
6. Record other observations you can make of your jars. What conclusions can you draw regarding the addition of various pollutants to water supplies?

TESTING FOR DISSOLVED OXYGEN IN WATER

BACKGROUND

The water ecosystem is a dynamic one that fluctuates from too much oxygen to not enough. Oxygen is produced by the green plants during periods of sunlight. If there is an excessive increase in algae growth, much oxygen is produced. This increase in algae resulting in an *algae bloom* is caused by an increase of organic matter, phosphates and nitrates. The organic matter can come from fecal material or decaying plants and animals. The phosphates come from fertilizer and detergents; the nitrates, from fertilizers.

Although plants produce oxygen during the photosynthetic process, they also respire and use up much of the oxygen produced. The processes of decomposition and decay also consume oxygen. As in aerobic respiration, oxygen combines with the organic compounds to break them down. The resultant products are carbon dioxide (CO_2), water (H_2O), and heat energy.

$$HO - \overset{\overset{O}{\parallel}}{C} - \overset{\overset{H}{|}}{\underset{\underset{H}{|}}{C}} - \overset{\overset{H}{|}}{\underset{\underset{H}{|}}{C}} - \overset{\overset{H}{|}}{\underset{\underset{H}{|}}{C}} - \overset{\overset{H}{|}}{\underset{\underset{H}{|}}{C}} - \overset{\overset{H}{|}}{\underset{\underset{H}{|}}{C}} - H \quad + \quad O_2 \longrightarrow \quad CO_2 \quad + H_2O \quad + \quad E$$

organic compound   + oxygen yields carbon dioxide + water + energ

Anaerobic bacteria decompose organic matter also and as the DO decreases, the anaerobic bacteria become more active. The products of anaerobic decomposition are methane gas and active hydrogen.

$$HO - \overset{\overset{O}{\parallel}}{C} - \overset{\overset{H}{|}}{\underset{\underset{H}{|}}{C}} - \overset{\overset{H}{|}}{\underset{\underset{H}{|}}{C}} - \overset{\overset{H}{|}}{\underset{\underset{H}{|}}{C}} - \overset{\overset{H}{|}}{\underset{\underset{H}{|}}{C}} - \overset{\overset{H}{|}}{\underset{\underset{H}{|}}{C}} - H \quad + \text{ Enzymes} \longrightarrow \quad CH_4 \quad + \quad H$$

organic compound   + enzymes yields methane + active hydrogen

The hydrogen formed quickly combines with nitrogen (N_2) forming ammonia gas (NH_3), sulfur (S) forming sulfite (SO_3) or sulfate (SO_4) ions or hydrogen sulfide (H_2S). When these products and other gases reach certain proportions—80% CH_4, 1.2% NH_3 and H_2S, 18% CO_2—their odors can be detected.

Pollutants and temperature influence the DO content. Cold water can hold more dissolved oxygen than warm water. As the molecules of water spread upon warming, the oxygen escapes into the atmosphere.

McKee and Wolff determined the minimum dissolved oxygen required for survival of fish within an 84 hour period. (Chart No. 4)

Chart No. 4
Minimum Dissolved Oxygen Required for
Survival of Fish for 84 Hours*
(Milligrams per liter)

Fish variety	minimum concentration required for survival at indicated temperature		
	10 °/C	16 °C/	20 °C/
Rainbow Trout	1.89	3.00	2.64
Perch	1.05	1.34	1.25
Roach	0.65	0.71	1.42
Mirror Carp	0.48	0.73	3.74
Tench	0.35	0.54	—
Dace	—	1.14	—
Bleak	—	1.50	—

Activity 1:   DETERMINING THE DISSOLVED OXYGEN (DO) CONTENT IN WATER

MATERIALS (per class)

Prepare the necessary reagents as follows for the Winkler Method of DO Determination.

1. Manganous sulfate. Weigh out 480 grams of $MnSO_4 . 4H_2O$ or 400 grams of $MnSO_4 .2H_2O$. Pour it into a 1 liter volumetric flask and bring it up to volume with distilled water.
2. Alkaline iodide. Weigh out 500 grams of NaOH (or 700 grams KOH) and 135 grams NaI (or 150 grams KI) per liter of distilled water.
3. Concentrated sulfuric acid. Specific gravity 1.83—1.84. Approximately 36 Normal H_2SO_4. Use as it.
4. Sodium Thiosulfate:
   a. Stock, 0.1 Molar, weigh out 24.82 grams $Na_2S_2O_3.5H_2O$ and add enough water to make 1 liter. To preserve it, add 5 ml of ammonium chloride and chloroform per liter.
   b. Standard thiosulfate—0.025 Molar, Dilute 250 ml of Stock solution to 1 liter. Add 5 ml chloroform per liter. Make up

*Source: Resources Agency of California, State Water Quality Control Boards Water Quality Criteria, Jack E. McKee and Harold Wolff. Publ. 3-A, 1963, p. 181.

fresh 0.025M thiosulfate solution each time because it
deteriorates rapidly.

5. Soluble starch solution: 1% prepared fresh. Grind 1 gram
soluble starch in a little water to form a paste. Add 100 ml of
boiling distilled water.
Also have 250 ml ground glass, stoppered bottles for taking
samples and 3-10 ml graduated cylinders or 3-1 ml pipettes.

METHODS: Winkler Procedure

A. *In the Field:* (per student or team of 2 or 3 students)
1. Add 1 ml of manganous sulfate and 1 ml of alkaline iodide
to each 250 ml glass-stoppered sampling bottle.
2. Fill the bottles over the top so as not to trap air and stopper
tightly. Take samples early and late in the day, for example,
9:00 a.m., 11:00 a.m., 1:00 p.m., and 3:00 p.m.
3. Place thumb over the stopper and swing back and forth in an
arc to mix reagents with the water. Shake for 1 minute to
distribute the precipitate that forms.

B. *In the Laboratory:* (per student or team of 2 or 3 students)
4. Add 1 ml of 36 Normal H_2SO_4 slowly down the inside of the
bottle to acidify the mixture. Stopper carefully.
5. Shake again in the same manner until everything is
distributed evenly.
6. Measure out a calculated amount of the sample in a
graduated cylinder and transfer to a 400 ml beaker for
titration.

Calculation for step 6

Amt. of sample for titration $= 200$ ml $\times \dfrac{\text{original volume of sample (250 ml)}}{\substack{\text{original volume of sample (250 ml)}\\ \text{less total volume of reagent added}\\ \text{(2 mg) not corrected for acid.}}}$

7. Fill the volumetric burette with the 0.025 N thiosulfate and
titrate into the sample very carefully until the iodine fades to
a pale straw color.
8. Add 2ml of starch solution to the sample and titrate until the
blue just disappears. Be careful not to go beyond the end
point. (Molecular Iodine (I_2) has been reduced to the iodide
ion (I^-).
9. Record the amount of 0.025 N $Na_2S_2O_3$ that was used to
reach the end point. Since 1 ml of $Na_2S_2O_3$ is equivalent to
0.2 mg of oxygen, the number of milliliters of thiosulfate

solution used is equivalent to the mg/liter of dissolved oxygen (DO) if a volume of 200 ml of the original sample was titrated.

10. Record the milligrams per liter of DO in your sample.
11. Calculations for parts per million (ppm)
For a 250 ml bottle:

$$\frac{K}{\text{(constant)}} = \frac{\text{volume of bottle (250 ml)}}{\text{volume of bottle minus volume of reagents}}$$
$$(250 \text{ ml}) \quad - \quad (2 \text{ ml})$$

$$\text{ppm} = K \times 200 \times \frac{\text{volume of 0.025 N thiosulfate acid}}{\text{volume of sample titrated}}$$

(parts per million oxygen)

EVIDENCE OF EUTROPHICATION

BACKGROUND

Normal succession (the orderly and progressive changes that take place in nature) in bodies of water takes place gradually and over a long period of time. In fact, in natural areas untouched by man, it is difficult to find evidence of these changes within one's life time. When man, however, tampers with nature the process of succession is often accelerated. As bodies of water age, they become warmer and shallower. Both factors tend to increase the amount of living things in the water. When the productivity of the water has reached the adequate nourishment stage, the body of water is termed *eutrophic*. The process of increasing productivity is called *eutrophication*. When this process is speeded up by pollution far beyond normal succession rates, the body of water is doomed to an early death.

We can find evidence of rapid eutrophication caused by pollutants by examining the change in communities of plants and animals. For example, as lakes become shallower and warmer, fish preferring cold, deep waters move out, and fish preferring warm, shallow water move in. Thus whitefish, walleye, coho, salmon, trout, and lake herring (char) move out and are replaced by bass, pike and smelt. When eutrophication and pollution become more severe, sunfish, carp and catfish also move in.

Evidence of eutrophication can also be found by examining the animal populations on the floor of a body of water. As streams and lakes begin to fill in, the bed becomes covered with silt and mud. Burrowing animals requiring little oxygen begin to appear. Suggest to your students that they look for sludge worms (Tubifex), leeches, sow bugs (*Asellus* isodod), and bloodworms (*Chironomus* larva). They should also find the mosquito larva (*Culex*), the bee fly (robberfly or hover fly, *Eristalis*), and the mothfly (sewage fly, *Psychoda*). Although these animals require oxygen, they inhabit deoxygenated waters and survive there because of their ability to take in oxygen through air tubes protruding from their bodies.

The most obvious evidence of eutrophication is the presence of algae growth on a body of water. You might think that these tiny one-celled green plants would provide abundant oxygen and food for supporting life but, to the contrary, they block the penetration of light reducing the ability of water plants to carry on photosynthesis which produced food for them and oxygen for the animals. Algae grow in all water sources, ponds, lakes, ditches, puddles, ocean water and so on. The presence of algae in water is normal and under normal conditions, they *are* essential to life. It is only when there is an alga bloom or an overabundance of algae that they do damage.

Apparently, only certain kinds of algae can be used as indicators of pollution. Of the blue-green algae, *Anabaena, Aphanizomenon, Anacystis* and *Microcystis* are most common. Of the green algae, *Spirogyra* and *Chorella* are very tolerant of polluted water and the common flagellates, *Euglena* and *Chlamydomonas,* will live in ponds that are rich in organic matter. The presence of these algae and flagellates indicate rapid eutrophication is taking place.

Coliform bacteria and perhaps zooplankton also contribute to the eutrophication process and their presence indicates that the water is polluted.

KEY POINTS

Key Points and Activities

A checklist for determining whether or not rapid eutrophication is taking place as a result of pollution:

Evidence of Eutrophication

____perch	____bee fly
____bass	____moth fly
____pike	____Anabaena
____smelt	____Aphanizomenon
____sunfish	____Anacystis
____carp	____Microcystis
____catfish	____Spirogyra
____sludgeworm	____Chorella
____leech	____Euglena

Evidence of Eutrophication (continued)

_____ sow bug   _____ Chlamydomonas
_____ bloodworm   _____ Coliform bacteria
_____ mosquito larva   _____ Zooplankton (?)

GLOSSARY

bacteria — microscopic, one-celled, plant-like organisms belonging to the Kingdom Protista. Classified into four major groups according to their feeding habits: saprophytic, which feed on dead organic matter; commensal, non-parasitic bacteria which inhabit living systems; parasitic, which includes the pathogens, get their food from a living host; and autotrophs which produce their own food.

commensal (commensalism) — a simple type of interaction in which one organism benefits and the other is not harmed.

Eschericha coli — rod shaped bacteria 0.5 microns in diameter and 1.0 to 3.0 microns in length. May occur singly, in pairs and in short chains. Found in the large intestines of man and other animals. Assist the host in the breakdown of waste products of digestion.

pathogenic organism — a disease causing organism.

Winkler Method — a chemical procedure for determining the dissolved oxygen (DO) concentration in water.

BIBLIOGRAPHY

Ahrens, Maurice R., Norris F. Bush, and Ray K. Easley. *Living Chemistry.* Boston: Ginn and Company, 1961.

Andrews, William A. *A Guide to the Study of Environmental Pollution.* Englewood Cliffs, New Jersey: Prentice-Hall, Inc., 1972.

Blaustein, Elliott H. *Anti-Pollution Lab.* New York: Sentinel Book Publishers, Inc., 1972.

Bryan, Arthur H. and Charles G. Bryan. *Bacteriology: Principles and Practice.* College Outline Series. New York: Barnes & Noble, 1959.

Hach. *Simplified Tests for Water and Pollution Analysis.* Ames, Iowa: Hach Chemical Company, 1971.

Kelly, James and Harold Wengart. *Pollution — Man' Crisis: An Investigative Approach.* North Dakota Studies, 1971.

Laun, H. Charles. *The Natural History Guide.* Alton, Illinois: Alsace Books and Films, 1970.

Millipore, *Experiments in Microbiology.* Bedford, Massachusetts: Millipore Corp, 1963.

Rabinowitz, A. *Oceanography: An Environmental Approach to Marine Science.* Hoboken, New Jersey: Oceanography Unlimited. Inc., 1970.

Standard Methods for the Examination of Water and Waste Water, New York: American Public Health Association, Inc., 1969.

Storin, Diane. *Investigating Air, Land, and Water Pollution.* Bronxville, New York: Pawnee Publishing Company, Inc. 1971.

Wedberg, Stanley E. *Paramedical Microbiology.* New York: Reinhold Publishing Corporation, 1963.

Wisconsin Department of Public Instruction. *Pollution: Problems, Projects and Mathematics Exercises,* 1971.

7

Ways to Study the Land

OBSERVING THE TOPOGRAPHY OF THE LAND

BACKGROUND

Topography is the science which deals with mapping the surface features of the land. The surface or physical features of the land include hills, valleys, mountains, rivers, streams, lakes and so on. Geologists, engineers, surveyors, aviators, mountain climbers, cross country skiers and the like use topographic maps to study the land. These maps are relief maps in that they show elevations and depressions. They also show highways, railroads, bridges, water towers, beacons, weather stations and other man-made features within a particular region. Point out to your students some of the obvious reasons why topography is an important study and why topographic maps are useful and in some cases, as to the aviator, essential. Obtain some topographic maps from the United States Geological Survey and visit or write to your town's Zoning and Planning Department. You might also have your students search the library for examples of them in geography, social studies or geology books.

Have your students study the topographic maps of an area in your local region or one prepared by the U.S. Geological Survey (U.S.G.S.). The U.S.G.S. maps are usually constructed so that one inch or 2.5 cm equals one mile. They are usually printed in three to five colors. Roads, bridges, towers, houses and boundaries are usually in black and sometimes in red. Water areas are in blue, lines representing the elevation of the land surfaces are in brown, and timber or woodland areas on some maps are in green. Try to have your students identify these areas and help them interpret and use the key.

Contour lines are used to illustrate relief or the elevation of the land above sea level and have a value given in either feet or meters. The spaces between the contour lines are called *intervals*. Lines of latitude and longitude are used to locate a particular place on the map. *Lines of latitude* run east and west and are used to measure distance from the equator, which is at 0 degrees latitude to the South and North Poles. *Lines of longitude* run north and south and are used to measure distance from the prime meridian, which passes through the Greenwich Observatory in London, to the poles. Each degree of latitude and longitude is divided into 60 minutes (60') and each minute into 60 seconds (60"). Ask your students to find the key to the map and study it. Note also that direction is shown by arrows indicating true and magnetic north. The magnetic North or South Poles do not coincide with the geographical poles and, therefore, the angle between magnetic and true north varies from place to place.

As an introductory exercise, ask the students to describe the topography of the land in their own region. Are there hills, mountains, valleys, rivers, ponds or other distinctive surface features?

Activity 1:   PRACTICE MAKING TOPOGRAPHIC MAPS

MATERIALS (per student)

poster board or chart paper
brown crayon, felt pen, or brown pencil
play dough, clay or a potato
thumbtack
ruler

METHODS

1. Make play dough (see appendix for directions) out of salt, flour and water to the consistency for forming a model of a mountain. If you prefer, use clay, paper-mache, or carve a potato.
2. Place a thumbtack in the center of the bottom of your model.
3. Place the model on the poster board. Draw a line around the base.
4. Mark the center of your drawing to coincide with the center of your model.
5. Cut off the base of the mountain and measure the height of the piece cut.
6. Place the model in the center of the drawing again and draw a line around the new base. Record the distance between the lines as measured in #5 above. (Figure 7-1.)

Figure 7-1.

7. Repeat this procedure until you have reached the top of the mountain model.

Activity 2: GATHERING DATA FOR DRAWING A TOPOGRAPHIC MAP

MATERIALS (per team of 2 or 3 students)

5 tacks
   piece graph paper
   board the size of the graph paper
   string the length and width of graph paper
   straw
   protractor
   carpenter's level or medicine vial (filled with water or mineral oil)
2 wooden stakes

METHODS

Part I: *Outdoor Mapping*

1. Select an outdoor region near the school to map.
2. Tack a large piece of graph paper on a board.
3. Draw a baseline on the graph paper and record your key in the right hand corner. For example, you may wish to have 1 inch equal 1 foot (or 3 centimeters equal 1 meter).
4. Tie a string connecting two pencils long enough to reach the ends of the paper. Make sure the pencils are the same height so you can use them as sighting devices.
5. Using the scale on your paper as a reference, drive stakes into the ground representing your base line. Use the position of the stakes to sight the object on the land.
6. Beginning at the left stake, sight the object from this point with your mounted graph paper and pencils. Be certain your sights are level with the base of the object. Position each tree, flag pole,

bridge, road, building, mountain, and other objects on your graph paper.

7. Move to the right stake now and repeat the procedure until you have mapped everything in your defined region.

Part II: *Mapping the Contours of the Land*

1. First you will construct a simple sextant. A *sextant* is an instrument for measuring angular distances. Pin or tack a thin straw to the center of the base of the protractor so the straw will swivel and act as a pointer. Tack this assembly to the side of a carpenter's level. If you wish, you may use a very clean medicine vial filled with water or mineral oil. To be level, the bubble should be centered when the vial is placed on its side. Seal the vial with tape so it will not leak and tape the protractor to it.

2. Again, begin at the left stake, and sight the base of a land form through the straw making sure the bubble in your level is centered.

3. Now move the straw up until the top of the object is sighted. Record this number. (Suppose you have sighted a hill and found the angle to be 12°.)

4. From the left stake, measure the distance to the base of the hill. (Let's say the distance is 710 feet.) What is the height of the hill?

5. In order to solve this problem, you can use a Trigometric Table. Look up the tangent of sine 12°. A brief review of some trigometric functions should help.

In a right triangle:

$$\sin A = \frac{\text{side opposite angle A (a)}}{\text{hypotenuse (c)}}, \quad \sin A = \frac{a}{c}$$

$$\cos A = \frac{\text{side adjacent to angle A (b)}}{\text{hypotenuse (c)}}, \quad \cos A = \frac{b}{c}$$

$$\tan A = \frac{\text{side opposite angle A (a)}}{\text{side adjacent angle A (b)}}, \quad \tan A = \frac{a}{b}$$

6. The tangent of 12°, found in the Table, is 0.2126. When we place this number in the formula, we have:

$$\tan A \,(12° = 0.2126) = \frac{\text{side opp. angle A (a)}}{\text{side adj. angle A (b)}}$$
$$(710 \text{ ft.})$$

OR

$$0.2126 = \frac{a}{710 \text{ ft.}}$$
$$a = 710 \times 0.2126$$
$$a = 150.9 \text{ ft.}$$

Therefore, the height of the hill is 150.9 or 151 ft. (This problem can also be solved by similar triangles and proportions.)
7. Mark this height on your map in the location of the hill.
8. Make similar sights at varying heights of the hill and draw in the contours. Usually contour lines are spaced the same distance apart and represent definite distance intervals. For example, the contour interval of 1/2 inch may represent 10 feet. Decide what ratio you will use for your contour intervals and record this in your key.
9. Repeat the above for each object in the region you are mapping. Draw in the contour lines and record the elevations on your *topographic* map.

Activity 3: CONSTRUCTING A RELIEF MODEL FROM A TOPOGRAPHIC MAP

MATERIALS (per team of 2 or 3 students)

corrugated cardboard from a carton, or styrofoam
thumbtacks
straight (common) pins
topographic map
large piece of plywood or flat cardboard
paste

METHODS

1. Place your topographic map on the cardboard and secure it with tacks.
2. Find the largest contour line of a land form and prick holes through the line with a straight pin to outline it on the cardboard.
3. Remove the map and cut out the cardboard. Paste it on a piece of plywood or flat cardboard base.
4. Do the same for all the contours. Paste each cardboard cut-out on top of each other to show the elevation of each contour interval.
5. When your relief map is constructed, cover it with paper-mache, play dough (salt, flour and water) or modeling clay to make your map more realistic. Draw in the lakes and rivers and paint the model.

Before you leave this section, ask your students to describe what they have observed about the topography of the land in their region.

What are some of the major land forms mapped? How were these natural features formed? Why are the hills, valleys, streams, and so on, where they are? What has man done to change the topography of the natural features of the land? Has man improved the topography or has he marred the natural beauty? Have the students share their studies and maps with other classes of science, social studies, and mathematics, or plan the whole lesson as an interdisciplinary exercise.

EXAMINING LAND FORMATIONS

BACKGROUND

Basically, land formations are of three types: elevations, depressions and water areas. The surface of our planet is constantly exposed to two antagonistic forces, one constructive and the other destructive. Land forms are *built up* by volcanic action, folds, faults and deposition; they are *worn down* by erosion processes such as weathering, water activity, glaciers, and organisms. In order to identify each land form, it is necessary to investigate the origin and development of each land form. This goes beyond the scope of this book, however. Nevertheless, your students can examine some land forms and build models of basic formations in your region. Urge your students to think about where they live in relation to *elevations* (mountains, hills, volcanoes), *depressions* (valleys, pits, holes) and water (ponds, lakes, rivers, streams, ocean) and why they live where they do. Why was the school placed where it is? What were some of the geographical reasons for placing the business district in your area where it is? Why was the town laid out the way it is? What is the nature of the topography and how does it relate to the plants, animals and human beings living in the area? Has the topography influenced the way of life in this region? These questions can stimulate much discussion by you and your students. Invite social studies teachers and science teachers into your class to contribute to the class discussion before involving your students in the activities which follow.

Activity 1:   USING A STREAM TABLE

MATERIALS (per team of 2 or 3 students)

stream table or sand box or large plastic wash tub
varieties of sand, soil, clay, gravel, pebbles, rocks

water source (sprinkler or faucet or jug or hose)
large pail
tubing
large funnel
2 blocks of wood

METHODS

1. Prop your stream table on something so it will be tilted.
2. Pour all the sand, soil, clay, gravel, etc. into a pail. Add water and pour the contents into the stream table at the highest point and watch the contents flow to the bottom.
3. Using a hose, or funnel, pour more water in from the highest elevation. What do you observe?
4. Now sprinkle water over the surface of the contents and record your observations.
5. Examine your model for evidence of various land formations. Are there elevations—deltas, hills, mountains, plateaus, faults, folds, other? Are there depressions—holes, pits, caverns, fissures, gullies, gorges, valleys, terraces, potholes, canyons, plunging pools?
6. Identify the *watershed* area, that is, the area that would drain into the main stream and tributaries.
7. Identify the *flood plain,* that is, the area that would flood and act as a giant sponge to hold back the water when the rivers overflow.
8. Keeping the above in mind, pretend you are on the Town Planning and Zoning Board and have to recommend how this land should be developed. What factors must you consider? What advice would you give to a builder who wants to construct condominiums, cluster homes or multiple family dwellings in the area of the main river?

You will want to do some advanced planning before introducing the second activity to your students. You will have them role play in attempting to solve a proposed problem. Meanwhile, select one of the best stream table models in the class and hook it up to a continuous water source. Attach a hose to a faucet and let the water trickle slowly down the center of the stream table throughout the next activity. Attach a hose to the lower end and collect the runoff water in a large pail, or let it run out the door, window or down a drain.

Plant grass and some small plants at random in the soil of the stream table. When the soil has settled and the plants have grown, begin the following activity.

Activity 2:   DECISION MAKING SIMULATION GAME

MATERIALS (per class)

model of a river area   ⎫ obtain
information on local town government organization   ⎪ from
information on local town environmental regulations ⎬ town or city
information on building codes   ⎪ hall
                                                                              ⎭

METHODS

1. Form the following committees, departments, groups, etc. and randomly assign students to them.

   Local Chamber of Commerce
   Open-Space Construction Company
   Citizens for the Environment
   Town Surveyor
   Town Engineer
   Town Health Officer
   Town Planning and Zoning Commission
   Town Conservation Commission

2. *The Problem.* The Open-Space Construction Company wants to construct condominiums for 400 families in the river area (stream table model). They intend to pipe some of the small streams and to use some of the flood plain area for access roads and bridges. They also plan to install septic tanks, even though they will connect to the city water system.

   The Citizens for the Environment have gone to the Town Conservation Commission to fight the proposed construction.

3. Have the students in each group play the roles they have been assigned and to develop a case for or against the proposed construction plan. Encourage them to use the model to support their stand on the issue.

4. When each group has prepared its case, have them debate the problem by playing the roles at a mock public hearing. Let them elect their own moderator and establish their own procedural rules for this simulation.

MAKING PROFILES OF THE LAND

BACKGROUND

A *profile* of the land is a vertical section of soil and rock layers. Soil profiles are produced over a long period of time—over hundreds or thousands of years. The climate and weathering play a role in determining the rate at which soil profiles are developed. As rock material is broken down, various layers of soil called *horizons* are formed. Each horizon has its own characteristics or properties. The top horizon or the "A" horizon is topsoil and contains humus. The humus is produced by the action of microorganisms on dead plants and animals. During the decomposition process, certain bacteria convert nitrogen gas into a form that can be used by plants. Humus is a primary source of nitrogen and is therefore very valuable.

Topsoil horizons and substream horizons vary according to their location. One would expect the soil in a grassland to be different than that found in the forest and it is. The same is true of the substrata. Sometimes horizon "B" is a solid or consolidated bedrock. Other times horizon "B" will be a loose unconsolidated rock. Soils also differ in age. A mature soil will have many well defined horizons whereas an immature soil will have only a few, with indistinctive characteristics.

Profiles can also be seen in rock formations. You have to look for them in outcrops. *Outcrops* are rock formations at the earth's surface. These rocks are exposed to the surface and are not covered with soil and vegetation. *Exposures,* as they are also called, can be seen in stream beds, along highways where roads have been cut through hills and mountains, and quarries. As your students locate outcrops and study them, they will notice that the rocks are layered. These layers are called *beds.* The beds are discernible because they are separated by different rock types or planes of separation called *bedding planes.* The beds are formed by the deposition and cementing of sediment particles that eventually formed sedimentary rock.

Activity 1:   MAKING SOIL PROFILES

MATERIALS (per team of 2 or 3 students)

core sampler (peat corer), or construct a corer by placing one

pipe, approximately 1.828 meters or 6 ft. long, inside another. Place a pipe cap on the bottom of the inside pipe.
hammer or mallet to drive down the corer
flexible plastic wrap
2 doz. medicine vials with caps, or long plastic tubes, or stiff clear plastic
tape
felt pen
graph paper and mounting board

METHODS

1. Select various sites to take soil samples, A, B, C, etc. Select sites where you can predict you will get different soil profiles, such as from the top of a hill, at the bottom of a hill and so on. Try to find a natural area undisturbed by man.
2. Plunge the soil sampler into the ground. Hit it a few times with the hammer if necessary.
3. Extract the sample and expel the soil core onto plastic wrap.
4. Examine the sample.
   a. How many horizons are there?
   b. Starting at the top, describe each horizon.
   c. What does the soil in each horizon look like? Color?
   d. What is its texture? Is it granular? Is it fine? Is it course? Is it clay? Is it sandy?
   e. Is it dry or wet?
   f. How deep is the total sample?
   g. How deep is each horizon?
5. Record all your data in the field or wrap up the sample in the plastic wrap and take it back to the classroom.
6. Make a drawing of your soil sample to scale on the left side of a piece of graph paper.
7. Wrap the core sample in a long plastic tube, seal the ends and label each horizon. As an alternative, cut each horizon and separate it. Carefully fill a medicine vial with soil from each horizon, label it and tape it next to the scaled drawing on your graph paper.
8. Describe the soil in each horizon next to each sample on the right side of your graph paper. Mount the graph paper on a piece of cardboard as a permanent record. (Figure 7-2.)
9. Repeat the above with samples from other sites.
10. How do your soil samples compare? Do you have mature or immature soil profiles? Can you tell anything about the age of

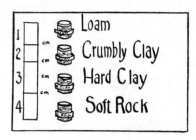

Figure 7-2. Soil Profile

the soil in each horizon of samples? Did you find fossils (hardened remains of plants and animals of another geological age as evidence of ancient life), or *artifacts* (objects made by man of a different era)?

Activity 2:   MAKING PROFILES OF OUTCROPS

MATERIALS (per class)

camera   clipboard
pencil   tape measure
graph paper   Jacob's staff

METHODS

1. Construct Jacob's staff to measure the horizontal and tilted layers of rock. Nail a 30.5 cm or a 1 foot board even with the top of a 5 foot or 1.52 meter board. (Figure 7-3.)

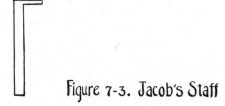

Figure 7-3. Jacob's Staff

2. Visit an outcrop area and photograph the rocks at a distance and close-up. Are the beds obvious? Are they tilted or horizontal? Are the beds uniform or do they differ in thickness? Can you see the bedding planes? Are there faults (breaks) in the rocks indicating movement?
3. Measure the thickness of the rock beds you can reach with your

tape measure. Sketch a profile (side view) of the rocks on your graph paper, record the measurements and describe the features of each bed. (Figure 7-4.)

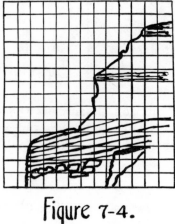

Figure 7-4.

LOOKING FOR EVIDENCE OF EROSION AND DEPOSITION

BACKGROUND

The study of geology is deeply concerned with the struggle between the external forces of erosion or wasting away and the internal forces which cause continental uplift. The agents of erosion are wind and water, and the cause of erosion by these agents is the downslope movements of material by gravity. Some of the internal causes of uplift are volcanoes, earthquakes, and the folded and tilted sedimentary rocks which were once under the sea.

Examples of erosion are many. Alert your students to some of the examples of mass wasting in your area. Look for rockfall, soil runoff by rain water and removal of topsoil or sand by the wind.

Large amounts of material are eroded by downslope movements called *creep, earthflow, mudflow* and *landslide.* Creep is when the downslope movement is slow and causes fence posts, trees and shurbs to bend as a result of the constant slow movement of surface material. When the amount of water increases, an earthflow results and more water will eventually cause various types of mudflow. Eventually, landslides of two types may occur. Landslides are *rockslides* when a mass of bedrock breaks loose and slides down a slope. The other type of landslide is called a *slump.* A slump usually develops when a strong resistant type rock, such as sandstone, is over a weak rock such as shale. The weaker rock slips beneath the stronger rock and causes the outer surface to slump. Have your students look for evidence of erosion along river banks and in the river bed. Check for potholes in the rock. Look for downcutting at the headwaters and determine the new and original profiles of the course of a stream. Look for flat-lying sedimentary rocks in mountains, banks, and road-cuts.

Wind can cause erosion by *deflation* (depression) and *abrasion* (sandblasting). Deflation can cause blowouts or hollows to form and can be seen in very dry areas void of vegetation such as in the desert. Abrasions can be seen on boulders and at the base of cliffs where wind-driven sand is blasted against them. The sand causes objects to become pitted and worn.

Glaciers have also contributed to the erosion of the land. Glacial erosion can change a V-shaped river valley into a U-shaped glacial valley. When glaciers have greater movement at their center than the outer parts, crevasses open up in the brittle ice.

Evidence of uplift, or the build-up of the land, can also be found. Have your students look for the build-up of materials at the foot of a steep slope as a result of rockfall. A similar build-up can be seen in streams where the stream undercuts the bank and part of the hillside slides into the river bed. Study the geologic work of the rivers as they erode, transport, and deposit soil and rock material. Look for deposits along the sides, build-up in the center, and delta formations at the mouths of rivers and streams. *Alluvial fans,* similar to deltas, are formed where streams flow out of the mountains into broad and flat valleys. There may also be evidence of levees in areas which have been flooded. As the water overflows a river bank and floods the flood plain, the water velocity is reduced and deposits are made near the river banks. These deposits form natural levees.

Wind can cause land build-up. It can blow soil, sand and dust against a wall or vegetation. It can also cause the formation of dunes. There are several basic types of dunes and some even form where there is only a small amount of sand.

Glaciers also deposit the debris they carry. When a glacier melts, it drops the material it is carrying. All types of glacial deposits are called *drift. Till* is the name given to ice deposited sediments.

Activity 1:   A FIELD TRIP IN SEARCH OF EVIDENCE FOR EROSION AND DEPOSITION

MATERIALS (per team of 2 or 3 students)

camera   felt pen
paper   clip board

METHODS

1. Do some studying in the library first on the causes of erosion and deposition. Take down some notes so you will recognize evidence of them in your surroundings.
2. Walk around the school and take photographs of examples of erosion and deposition. Record these on your note paper and describe the location for each example.
3. Extend your field trip to other areas where you would expect to find more evidence.
4. When you return to class, select a specific topic for further study related to erosion and deposition: volcanoes, earthquakes, glaciers and so on. Search the literature, obtain some visual aids and then report back to the class.

Activity 2:   EXAMINING TOPOGRAPHIC MAPS FOR EVIDENCE OF EXTERNAL AND INTERNAL FORCES WHICH HAVE SHAPED THE LAND

MATERIALS (per class)

topographical maps of shorelines, river valleys, craters, mountains, volcanoes, earthquake regions, etc.

METHODS

1. Examine the topographic maps for evidence of erosion of the land and discuss these in class. What forces caused the erosion?
2. Find areas where land has been built-up. What forces contributed to the uplifting of the land?
3. Locate crater lakes, volcanoes, volcanic mountains, glacial lakes, hanging valleys, mountain glaciers, canyons, alluvial fans and cones, streams, caves, natural levees, emerged and submerged shorelines, etc. Discuss these and what possibly caused them with other students.

GRAVEL PITS AND GLACIERS

We can see in a gravel pit today the work which a glacier can do over a long period of time. A gravel pit, or a quarry, is a large open hole in the side of a hill. There are many kinds of quarries: granite, marble and sandstone are examples. Like glaciers, machines break up large rocks into smaller ones and transport them from one place to another. If there is a rock quarry near your school, suggest to your students that they visit and watch the men at work quarrying and crushing the rock.

Much of the northern and northeastern part of the United States, Europe, and Asia contain land forms molded by glaciation. Glaciers are not solid masses of ice but consist of all types of debris, rocks, and snow. They also have small fissures or cracks in them and large crevasses. They may also harbor ice caves, ice bridges and irregular ice masses. A glacier is formed by the gradual accumulation of snow that is compressed. As snow falls upon a snow field, pressure increases and melts the snow. The cold, however, refreezes it and transforms granular snow to ice. The process continues until, under the weight and tremendous mass, the granular snow or ice begins to move.

A glacier is not a glacier until it starts to flow. As the glacier moves over the land it takes with it rocks and other debris and acts like a giant plow scraping the surface of the land. The rocks it carries scratch the surface of the land and leave grooves on the rocks as evidence of their passing. Depending upon the region in which you live, you may find evidence of glaciation.

Activity 1:   LOOKING FOR EVIDENCE OF GLACIATION

MATERIALS (per class)

resources on the natural history of your area
geological maps of your area
books on glaciers
films, filmstrips, etc. on glaciation

METHODS

1. Read and take notes on glaciers and how they may relate to the region in which you live.
2. View films, film loops and filmstrips on glaciers.
3. Visit a stream and examine the rocks in the area for evidence of glaciers having passed through the region. Do you find any glacial grooves in the rocks? Do you find samples of rock that are foreign to your area and may have been carried to your locality by a glacier?
4. Invite a geologist into your class and discuss your findings together.

MUD FLATS AND MARSHES

BACKGROUND

Some people think that mud flats and marshes are great for constructing boat marinas, for industrial development, for building houses with a view of the water, or for dumping solid wastes. Folks complain that these areas should be filled in or drained to cut down on the mosquito population, but in recent years, we have taken a more serious view of the uses and importance of mud flats and marshes. These areas are vital breeding grounds for fish, birds, wild animals, and crustacea. They are alive with plankton and other foods for water and land animals and the phytoplankton produce over 70% of all our oxygen.

There are fresh water and salt water marshes. A marsh is really a stage in the evolutionary process of succession. When ponds become filled in with vegetation, we call them *marshes*. In the normal process, it may take hundreds of thousands of years for a lake to become a marsh. A young pond, during the pioneer stage, has a sandy bottom and supports life that depends upon the relatively barren and open bottom. The first plankton communities might include bacteria, protozoa, algae, rotifers, and crustaceans. When the planktonic life is large enough to support larger forms of living things, blue gills, black bass, and speckled bullheads make nests on the sandy bottom. Other animals which inhabit a young pond include the snails, mussels, and the cadisfly larvae.

The next stage is called the *submerged vegetation stage.* This occurs after plants and animals have died and decayed and have formed humus on top of the sandy bottom. A large, branching algae begins to grow called *Chara* which serves as a resting and hiding place for the animals. Dragonfly and mayfly numphs burrow in the muddy bottom and small crustacea and a few crayfish can usually be found. Most of the animal forms are those which are dependent upon the submerged vegetation and are independent of the bottom and surface growth.

The *emerging vegetation* stage is the third phase of succession. Bivalve mollusks burrow in the mud and hide in the vegetation. Lung breathing snails are present and so are diving beetles and other carnivorous insects which feed on the aquatic larvae. Annelid worms and leeches can also be found in the mud.

After a time, more plants and animals die and build up more humus on the bottom and more algae grow on the surface, closing in the large areas of open water. If this stage is reached, and the covering is mainly grasses and sedges, a *marsh* has been formed. On the other hand, if the covering includes trees like the cypress or tamarack, a *swamp* has been formed.

Salt water marshes are deep, shallow, or very shallow, depending upon the depth of the peat and sediments. There are also *estuarine marshes* which are located at the mouths of rivers entering the ocean. *Tidal marshes,* those reached by salt water, can be classified as such according to the plants that grow in them. You will want to have the students write to your State's Department of Environmental Protection and request information on Public Acts that may have been passed for the preservation of wetlands, tidal marshes, and estuarine systems. This information will be helpful to you and your students in studying these areas.

When studying the marshes, you will also want to pay some attention to the properties of the sediments and the traditional elements of soil classification. These include the acidity of the soil, the salinity, organic matter, depth of the peat and sediments, size of the particles and the clay minerals.

Activity 1:   FINDING EVIDENCE FOR A STAGE OF SUCCESSION IN A FRESH WATER MARSH

MATERIALS (per class)

hip boots
bottom dredge
dip nets
books on the identification of fresh water marsh plants and animals

METHODS

1. Wearing boots, collect samples of plant and animal life in the marsh with a bottom dredge and a dip net.
2. Store them in plastic containers until you can sort them in class. Keep in a cool place during storage.
3. As soon as possible, examine the specimens and try to identify your plants and animals.
   Do you have bivalve mollusks?
   Do you have lung breathing snails?
   Have you found carnivorous insects such as the diving beetle?
   Do you have Annelid worms, leeches?
   Is the bottom muddy?

Have you found larvae in your bottom samples?
Did you find many algae covering the water?
Were there only a few open water surfaces?
Was the ground covering mainly grasses and sedges?

4. After answering the questions above and others you may have thought of, what conclusion can you draw from your evidence regarding the stage of succession of your pond or fresh water marsh? Does it appear that indeed, your study was of a fresh water marsh?

Activity 2:   GATHERING DATA ON A SALT WATER MARSH

MATERIALS (per class)

peat sampler
plastic bags for soil samples

METHODS

1. Thrust the peat sample into the marsh soil as far as it will go. Measure the depth. Repeat this process in various locations in the marsh. (The depth of organic and inorganic layers in a marsh may range from 1 foot or .304 meters to 33 feet or 10.03 meters.)
2. Open the peat sampler and place the samples in plastic bags and close them with the wire covered twists to retain the moisture. Save for tests back in the classroom and laboratory.

Activity 3:   TESTING THE pH OF THE MARSH SOIL

MATERIALS (per class)

liquid Litmus indicator or Hydrion papers
spot plate
medicine dropper
spatula
distilled water
glass rod

METHODS

1. Scoop a little of the soil sample onto the spatula and place it in the depression of the spot plate.

2. Add one or two drops of distilled water and one or two drops of Litmus (or test with the Hydrion paper).
3. Stir and wait to see if there is a color change. (Litmus is red in acid, pink when neutral and blue in base. The pH range of Litmus is from 5.5-8.0.)
Is your sample acidic, neutral or basic? (The pH of coastal marshes is usually slightly acidic. Knowing the pH is important in determining whether or not there is salt or fresh water present, whether or not there are many shells neutralizing the acid due to their alkalinity, or whether or not there are sulfides present.)
4. Dry out the soil samples and test the pH again after 18 days.

Activity 4:   TESTING THE AMOUNT OF ORGANIC MATTER

MATERIALS (per student)

crucible   spatula
propane burner   balance

METHODS

1. Weigh out a sample of soil that has been thoroughly dried.
2. Place it in a crucible and apply the flame of the propane burner to it. Burn the organic matter away.
3. Let the crucible cool and weigh it again.
4. Calculate the percentage of organic matter per gram of sample. Suppose you weighed out a 5 gram dried soil sample and after burning the organic matter away, you had only 1.5 grams left. This would mean that 70% of your original sample contained organic matter.

$$5x \quad = \quad 3.5 \text{ grams}$$
$$x \quad = \quad \frac{3.5}{5}$$
$$x \quad = \quad .70 \text{ or } 70\% \text{ organic matter}$$

Activity 5:   A ROUGH DETERMINATION OF SALT CONTENT

MATERIALS (per student)

evaporating dishes or saucers
balance

METHODS

1. Weigh an evaporating dish.
2. Fill evaporating dish with your water sample. Weigh evaporating dish and water sample.
3. Let stand to evaporate. Place on a radiator or under a heat lamp to speed up evaporation.
4. After a day or two, examine your evaporating dish. Is there evidence of salt crystals?
5. Weigh the evaporating dish again and calculate the amount of salt in the sample as above. Don't forget to subtract the weight of the dish.

Suppose the dish weighed 5 grams and with the water sample, it weighs 7 grams. This means the sample weighs 2 grams. If, after evaporation, the dish plus the crystals weighs 5.5 grams, the crystals then, weigh 0.5 grams. Therefore, 25% of the sample was salt.

$$2x = 0.5$$
$$x = \frac{0.5}{2}$$
$$x = .25 \text{ or } 25\% \text{ salt}$$

Activity 6:   PARTICLE SIZE

MATERIALS (per team of 2 or 3 students)

sifting containers of various gauges, or mesh cloths of various hole size
several tumblers to hold the sifted soil

METHODS

1. Sift the dry soil sample and separate it by particle size.
2. Estimate the amount of each size in relation to one another.
   Interpretation
   1. Sediments with much silt and clay have a greater chemical activity than sand and gravel.
   2. Silt and clay are instable and impermeable.
   3. Sand lends strength and permeability.
   4. Silt and clay are deposited by slow moving rivers and tides.
   5. Sand and gravel are deposited by fast moving rivers and glaciers.
3. What can you say about your samples?

VOLCANOES AND MOUNTAINS

BACKGROUND

Volcanic action helps to shape the surface of the earth because, when the pressure of molten rock and gases forces a break in the rock at the earth's crust, the lava is thrown out and eventually cools on the surface. If lava has a low angle of rest before it solidifies, the volcano is one which flows quietly and builds up a broad mound. The formation looks like a Greek shield and hence, the name *shield volcano*. If the lava has a high angle of rest, the lava falls close to the opening and forms a cinder cone. Other times, the lava is thrown up in globs, and falls in a semiliquid state on the steep sides, forming a strong volcanic wall. These are called *spatter cones*.

Some volcanoes are active and continue to spew lava while others are inactive. Some of the inactive volcanoes are extinct or paid out while others are just dormant. It is difficult to tell which ones are truly extinct. Some may be plugged with cold lava and will explode when it is least expected.

Many mountains are formed by volcanic action which uplifts the rock from under the earth's surface. Mountains are also formed by faulting (breaking) and folding of rock. The formation of mountains reflects the unstable conditions of the earth in these regions. Mountain areas are characterized by high elevations and only a little level land.

Activity 1: BUILDING MOUNTAINS

MATERIALS (per class)

    clay of various colors
2 wooden blocks

METHODS

1. Roll out the clay so you have layers of different colors.
2. Place one layer upon another. This will represent the rock layers.
3. Place a block of wood on the top of each end of the clay and gently push them toward one another. This will demonstrate how pressure causes the rock layers to bend and form hills and mountains. As rocks bend they do so in "A" shaped forms called *anticlines* and in "S" shaped curves called *synclines*.

4. Apply more pressure and eventually the clay will crack simulating faults and will also fold.
5. Now with your hand, apply pressure to the top of your model. What happens? How could you cause uplifting of the land and illustrate it using your model?
6. Flatten out your clay layers again. With the blocks of wood placed on the ends, this time pull them apart gently. This will show you what happens during an earthquake. The earth shifts and stretches apart.

Activity 2:   BUILDING A VOLCANO

MATERIALS (per class)

powdered asbestos*   piece of tubing
large funnel   bicycle pump

METHODS

1. Make a water and asbestos paste and coat the outside of the funnel to simulate a volcano. Let dry.
2. Attach the tube to a bicycle pump and insert the tube under the inverted funnel. Pour powdered asbestos into the cone and mount it around the opening.
3. Pump a stream of air up through the inverted funnel. What do you observe? Although you are not applying heat and pressure, this will illustrate how erupting volcanic gases will scatter ash and pumice over the land from below the earth's surface.
4. Think of other ways you might build a model of a volcano. What is a geyser? Do a study of the number and types of volcanoes and geysers there are in the world and where they are located.

FIELDS AND FORESTS

BACKGROUND

The relationship of fields and forests is cyclic and changes occur over a long period of time due to normal succession. At the risk of oversimplifying, let's say that a field is any land area free of buildings and tall trees and a forest is any land area with predominately many large trees. The orderly and progessive changes that take place in the

*Powdered asbestos can be obtained from a plumbing or heating supply store.

communities of plants and animals on a particular tract of land or water area over the years is called *succession.* Succession is cyclic in that if left undisturbed, an area that was once a forest will become a forest again in time. Primary succession can take place from areas that are devoid of soil and organisms. Eventually, as soil and organic material accumulate, small plants will grow and animals start to move in. As this process continues, one kind of plant and animal replaces another until a dynamic equilibrium, called a *climax,* is reached. Secondary succession takes place in areas where previous communities already existed but for some reason, perhaps due to lumbering, fire, grazing, cultivation or construction, the area was disturbed and succession was set back. Evidence of secondary succession can be seen in a disturbed field within a twenty year period. You and your students might find a moderately grazed field with tree stumps in it. In ten years the field may be covered with low shrubs, and in twenty years there may be white pine and aspen trees growing on the land. This is evidence of the forest reclaiming the land. Encourage your students to look for places where man has abandoned the land and successional changes are apparent. If no abandoned land is available try to locate a film dealing with succession, especially in fields and forests.

Activity 1:   LOOKING FOR EVIDENCE OF SUCCESSION

MATERIALS (per class)

reference books on aquatic and terrestrial succession
keys on plant and animal identification
camera
paper and clip board

METHODS

1. Read and study about the different stages of succession.
2. Become familiar with the vegetation indicative of a particular community and successional stage.
3. Locate a site and evaluate the stage of succession. What stages do you think were present prior to the present stage? What do you predict will follow if the site is left undisturbed?
4. Locate and photograph sites that appear to have been undisturbed by man or fire.
5. Locate and photograph sites which obviously have been disturbed by man or fire and photograph them.

6. Try to find sites showing different stages of succession and photograph them making a pictorial story of the process.

KEY POINTS

Key Points and Activities

1. Review the following terms and use them in your class discussions:

topography	erosion
land formations	continental uplift
water shed	volcano
flood plain	earthquake
land profiles (soil and rock)	glacier
humus	quarry
outcrop	marsh
bed and bedding plane	swamp
soil horizons	mountain
faults and fold	succession
	climax

2. Make up some simulation games where you can role-play in discussing problems associated with man's use of the land. Use your previous studies to support opposing positions.
3. Develop a pictorial story of man's use and abuse of the land using photographs, slides, transparencies or drawings.
4. Identify a land problem in your town, do the research on it, run your tests and prepare your case based on the evidence you have found and present it to the proper pressure group or governmental department.

GLOSSARY

alluvial fan — deposit of materials at the base of a mountain stream.
bedding planes — interface areas when one rock bed abutts another.
beds — layers of rocks.
canyon — a long narrow valley between high cliffs.
cavern — a large hollow space inside the earth.
consolidated bed rock — solid rock usually found beneath the loose layers of earth but occasionally occuring as outcrops.
contour lines — symbols used on topographic maps to signify height and shape of elevations.
creep — a constant, slow, downslope movement of surface soil, resulting in the tilting of trees and other upright objects.

crevasse — a deep crack in a glacier.

delta — a triangular deposit of soil at the mouth of some rivers.

depressions — hollows or low places below the level of the earth's surface.

elevation — height of surfaces above the earth or above sea level.

erosion — the natural breaking down and wearing away of the surface by water, wind or ice.

fault — a fracture or break with accompanying movement resulting in dislocation of rock layers and mineral deposits.

flood plain — area surrounding rivers and lakes which normally hold flood waters.

fold — an overlapping of layers of bedrock created by a great force causing a sideward shift.

glaciation — a change in the landscape features caused by the movement of a glacier.

glacier — a large mass of ice and snow moving slowly down a mountain.

gully — a long, narrow, deep hollow worn in the earth by a stream.

horizons — distinctive layers of soil.

humus — soil containing organic material.

land formations — three types: elevations, depressions and water areas.

land profile — a vertical section of soil and rock layers.

latitude — distance north or south from the equator, measured in degrees.

longitude — measured in degrees east or west from the prime meridian.

moraine — ridge of rock and gravel piled up ahead of a glacier.

outcrops — rock formations that protrude above the earth's surface.

plankton — minute floating organisms in a body of water which serve as food for larger animals.

phytoplankton — plant plankton.

pot holes — round depressions made by the abrasion of rocks swirling around the surface of a fast moving stream.

soil profile — a vertical section of soil from the surface down through the horizons that exhibits different observable characteristics.

topography — science which deals with mapping the surface features of the land.

unconsolidated earth — the loose layers of earth above the bedrock layer.

watershed — areas which drain into streams and eventually into the same main river.

zooplankton — animal plankton.

BIBLIOGRAPHY

Blough, Glenn O., and Julius Schwartz. *Elementary School Science and How to Teach it.* New York: Holt, Rinehart and Winston, 1964.

Buchsbaum, Ralph, and Mildred Buchsbaum. *Basic Ecology.* Pittsburgh: Boxwood Press, 1957.

Earth Science Curriculum Project, *Investigating the Earth.* Boston: Houghton-Mifflin Company, 1967.

Hone, Elizabeth B., Alexander Joseph, Edward Victor, and Paul F. Brand-wein. *A Sourcebook for Elementary Science.* New York: Harcourt, Brace & World, Inc., 1962.

Lemkin, William. *Visualized General Science.* New York: Oxford Book Company, 1964.

Lounsbury, John F., and Lawrence Ogden. *Earth Science.* New York: Harper & Row Publishers, 1969.

Reid, George K. *Ecology of the Intertidal Zones.* Chicago: Rand McNally and Company, 1967.

Smith, Robert L. *Ecology and Field Biology.* New York: Harper & Row, Publishers, 1966.

Thurber, Walter A., and Robert Kilburn. *Exploring Earth Science.* Boston: Allyn and Bacon, Inc., 1970.

8

Tips on Studying Rocks and Minerals

A large portion of the abiotic environment is made up of rocks and minerals, and as has been said before, the environment consists of both living and non-living components. Rocks and minerals determine, to a certain extent, which life forms can exist in particular areas.

FACTORS DETERMINING THE WAY ROCKS AND MINERALS ARE FORMED

BACKGROUND

Before you begin this study with your students, be sure they understand the meaning of a few basic terms such as *mineral* and *rock.* A *mineral* is a chemical element such as carbon (C) or gold (Au). A mineral can also be compounds of two or more elements such as halite which is natural sodium chloride (NaCl), and quartz which is silicon dioxide (SiO_2). A *rock* is made of various minerals and is the solid form, or building unit, of the earth's crust or of the lithosphere. Rocks can be found almost everywhere. The smallest rocks are sand. Larger ones are called pebbles and stones. Big rocks are called boulders. Minerals can be found on top of the ground or under the ground. They may be found in layers or in large deposits in one place. Many minerals are found in ores and are mined, such as iron, coal, silver and copper. Minerals are also found in the sea. Salt, iodine, manganese and magnesium are just a few.

The basic factors that determine the way rocks and minerals are formed are temperature, pressure, location, and weathering. There is molten magma deep in the earth where it is very hot. Sometimes this

131

magma reaches the surface, cools, and forms rock; other times it cools beneath the surface. Other rocks are formed by layering under pressure. For example, every day mud, sand and rock are carried to the sea by rivers and streams. The rocks sink first because they are heaviest, then the sand and finally the mud sinks to the bottom forming sediment. As the layers build up, so does the pressure and the particles stick together to form rock. This process can also occur on land especially in regions of volcanoes. Volcanic dust settles and layers of rock are formed. Anything can fall one upon the other to form layers and, under the proper conditions of temperature and pressure, rocks are made. For instance, when shell fish die, their shells are deposited on the ocean bottom and eventually turn into limestone.

Rocks can come from other rocks and again, depending upon the temperature, pressure, location, and weathering, rocks can, and do, change from one kind to another. The new rocks do not resemble the old for they change in form and color.

Since rocks are made of minerals, the mineral content of the rocks will reflect the presence of certain chemical elements available when the rock was formed. Have your students perform the following activities.

Activity 1:   MAKING ARTIFICIAL ROCK

MATERIALS (per student)

1 jar—plus screw cover   sand
 mud   pebbles

METHODS

1. Fill a large jar 1/3 full with pebbles, sand and mud in equal amounts.
2. Fill up to 2/3 with water.
3. Screw on jar cover and shake vigorously.
4. Let stand until the next day.
5. Observe how the particles have settled in the jar. Record what you see.
6. Pack your soil several times each day with a flat object. Continue to do so for about two weeks.
7. After two weeks, carefully remove your artificial rock made from sediment. Try to remove it in one piece if possible.
8. Examine it with a hand lens or under a stereoscope. Draw, label, and describe what you see.
9. Did you in fact make an artifical rock? Explain.

Activity 2:   MAKING SILICA(SILICON DIOXIDE), SiO$_2$

MATERIALS (per student)

1 small shallow can or metal jar lid
sodium silicate ("water glass"—NaSiO$_3$ and H$_2$O)
dilute (1:1) Hydrochloric Acid (HCl)
Bunsen burner, alcohol lamp or hot plate
ring stand
asbestos pad
10 ml graduated cylinder or 5 ml pipette

METHODS

1. Deliver 3 ml sodium silicate into the can or lid.
2. Add 6 ml dilute HCl carefully. Observe what happens. The product of the reaction is called silica gel.
3. Place the container of silica gel over a flame and heat to drive out the water.
4. Observe what happens to the silica gel as it turns into non-crystalline silica.
5. Let the silica cool. Examine with a hand lens, then look at bits of it under a microscope. Describe.
6. Test the hardness of the silica by rubbing it on a piece of glass.
7. What factors determined the formation of your "rock"?

Activity 3:   STUDYING THE FORMATION OF ROCK BY ANALOGY

MATERIALS (per student)

paper cup
coarse sand
Epsom salt (magnesium sulfate, MgSO$_4$)

METHODS

1. Add some Epsom salt to a jar of water and shake vigorously. Add more, and shake until no more will dissolve. Heat and add more Epsom salt and let stand overnight.
2. The next day, add more Epsom salt to the solution to be sure it is saturated, that is when no more solute will dissolve in the solvent.
3. Fill a paper cup 1/4 full of coarse sand.
4. Add the saturated Epsom salt solution to the sand to cover it.

Mix well and let stand until dry or gently heat it or place under a light or on the radiator to speed up evaporation.

5. After the mixture of sand and Epsom salt has dried, cut away the paper cup and examine the "rock" that has formed.

6. Examine the rock with a hand lens. How does it resemble a rock formed in nature?

7. What is holding the sand together?

8. In what ways does this procedure resemble, or is "analogous" to the conditions in nature?

RECOGNIZING IGNEOUS, SEDIMENTARY AND METAMORPHIC ROCK FORMS

BACKGROUND

Most objects, living and nonliving, are classified according to their common characteristics or properties. Rocks, on the other hand, are classified according to their origin. *Igneous* rocks are those produced below the surface of the earth's crust. These rocks were formed under high temperature and pressure and, at one time, were in the molten or liquid state. They are often amorphous in structure and appear to be homogeneous throughout. Granite is a good example of an igneous rock. It is light colored with quartz (SiO_2) and feldspar ($KAlSi_3O_8$), and speckled with bits of mica, $K(MgFe)_3AlSi_3O_{10}(OH)_2$.

Granite was formed below the earth's surface as the magma cooled. Another common igneous rock is basalt. Basalt is formed from the cooling of black lava above ground. Basalt, like granite, is used in constructing roads, sidewalks and buildings. Another surface forming rock is obsidian. Obsidian is formed when lava cools rapidly. The Indians found this natural glass of many colors to be extremely useful. They made arrow and spear points and colorful jewelry from obsidian.

Sedimentary rocks are formed at the earth's surface. Sedimentary rocks have distinctive characteristics. They are often stratified, have cemented-grain textures, and contain a high percentage of precipitates which readily dissolve in water such as limestone, rock salt, and gypsum, or contain organic material such as coal. Materials which have been deposited by wind, rain, snow or death eventually form sediments on the surface of the earth. As time goes on, these sediments build up and the pressure of layers of sediment cause the sedimentary rock to form. Any deposit, such as salt after water evaporates at the edge of the Great Salt Lake, will become sedimentary rock.

Eventually sand will become sandstone. Sandstone is a building material and comes in many colors. The old brownstone houses were made of brown sandstone and hence the name, "brownstone." Evidence of layering or bedding can be found in most sedimentary rock deposits. Shale, formed from clay, is a good example of this. Shale resembles sheets of clay which have been cemented together.

Conglomerate and limestone are two more examples of sedimentary rocks. Conglomerate looks like peanut brittle with various pebbles cemented together. Limestone is light in color and smooth in texture. It is formed from sea shells and skeletons of tiny marine animals.

Metamorphic rocks are those which have been changed from one kind of rock to another. The change comes about by conditions deep in the earth's crust but not by melting. Metamorphic rocks show evidence of the changes that took place. Sometimes traces of layering, streakiness, shearing or distortion can be found. If the rock doesn't seem to be igneous or sedimentary, it perhaps is metamorphic.

Examples of metamorphic rocks are gneiss, marble, slate and schist. Gneiss has alternating light and dark bands of varying thicknesses. Marble comes in variated patterns and colors. Slate is smooth and consists of thin hard sheets pressed together. Schist consists of very thin bands. The crystals in schist can be seen with the naked eyes where as a hand lens must be used to see the crystal in slate. Often some of these forms are mixed together. For example, mica and schist are often found in the same rock.

It is believed that the earth's crust is about 4,000 million years old and therefore, it is unlikely that any of the original crust exists today. There is evidence that the rock-sediment-rock cycle or the rock-magma-rock cycle have taken place many times every few hundred million years.

As a teacher, you will want your students to become more familiar with rocks and therefore, it is suggested that they do some basic study activities. If you have access to a rock collection, this would help immensely. Perhaps you or your students know of a rock collector or geologist who would be willing to speak to the class.

Activity 1:   EXAMINING SEDIMENTARY, IGNEOUS AND METAMORPHIC ROCKS

MATERIALS (per class)

set or sets of the 3 kinds of rocks

charts and books on rocks
hand lens (per child) or stereoscopes

METHODS

1. Examine one rock at a time with the hand lens. For closer examination, view it under the stereoscope.
2. Write "Rock #1" in your notebook and describe the rock the best you can.

a. What color is it?
b. What is its texture? (How does it feel?)
c. Is it shiny or dull?
d. Is it hard or soft?
e. Can you break it?
f. Does it have an odor?
g. Do you think it is a sedimentary, igneous or metamorphic rock? What evidence do you have for your choice?

3. Go on to another rock sample and repeat #2 above.
4. When you have examined all your rock samples, try to determine if any of them are among the following major specimens:

Sedimentary	Igneous	Metamorphic
sandstone	granite	slate
limestone	basalt	schist
shale	obsidian	marble
conglomerate	diorite	quartzite
dolomite	felsite	serpentine
	trap rock	
	pumice	

Activity 2:   STARTING A ROCK COLLECTION

MATERIALS (per student)

canvas collecting bag, heavy plastic bag, old large shoulder pocketbook, or heavy paper bag
prospector's pick or hammer
chisel or old screwdriver
cigar boxes, shoe boxes or other appropriate container
cotton to use for lining the specimen boxes
masking tape for labeling rock specimens
notebook
3" x 5" file cards

METHODS

1. Collect your specimens in various places—open fields, wooded areas, mountains, open pits, mines, lakes, rivers, seashore, and where there is digging or construction taking place.
2. Collect as many different kinds of specimens as possible. Don't take more than two or three samples of the same rock. (You will need some extra specimens for future activities.)
3. If you find a large rock, chip off pieces with your screwdriver and hammer.
4. Place a number on each specimen by affixing a small piece of masking tape to the rock.
5. Record the number in your notebook. Also record the exact location including the city and state, the date you found it and, if you know it, the name of the rock.
6. After you have collected all the rocks you want for your "starter" collection, return to the laboratory for testing and positive identification.
7. Line your specimen boxes with cotton and place all the sedimentary rocks in one, your igneous rocks in another and your metamorphic rocks in still another box. Label the boxes as to the type of rocks. Keep an additional box for your unknown types.
8. After you have identified each rock, write the numbers you have given the rocks and their names on a 3" x 5" card and paste this "key" to identification on the top of the box.
9. Later, when you have a sizable collection, you may wish to have a card file for easy reference.

WAYS OF IDENTIFYING ROCK-FORMING MINERALS BY CHARACTERISTICS

BACKGROUND

Rocks are made up of minerals and sometimes a variety of minerals will be present in one piece of rock. Mica is often associated with the metamorphic rock schist. Mica is the chemical, $K(MgFe)_3$ $AlSi_3O_{10}(OH)_2$. Feldspar is often found in the igneous rock granite One type of feldspar has the chemical formula, $KAlSi_3O_8$. Sometimes minerals will forms rocks by themselves. For example, quartz, or SiO_2, forms it own rock and is found in various colors depending upon the impurities that are locked within the crystal. Diamond, which is a gem stone, is the element carbon. It is a gem stone because diamonds are hard to find, they are rare. and they can be polished to a high brilliance. For centuries men have considered gem stones to be of great value.

Rock-forming minerals are identified by their physical and chemical properties. Your students may recall that *physical properties* refer to the way something looks, feels, smells, and so on. In other words, they are the characteristics that are perceived through the senses. How does it taste? What does it feel like or what is its texture? Is it light in weight or heavy compared to something else? Does it have an odor? What does it look like? What does it sound like? Specifically, when we refer to the physical properties of rocks and minerals, we are interested in hardness, specific gravity, cleavage, structure, fracture, crystal shape, color, luster, transparency, and streak. These properties give clues to a mineral's identity.

Chemical properties refer to the way something reacts with something else, that is, the way in which a mineral changes chemically when the mineral reacts with elements or compounds. When substances react chemically they form a new substance which does not resemble the original substances at all. For example, when iron is burned, it combines chemically with oxygen to form a new product, rust, which does not resemble either iron or oxygen gas. The reaction follows:

$$4\,Fe \quad + \quad 3O_2 \quad \xrightarrow[\text{yields}]{\triangle\ \text{Heat}} \quad 2Fe_2O_3$$

$$\text{iron} \quad + \quad \text{oxygen gas} \qquad\qquad \text{iron oxide}$$
$$\text{(rust)}$$

In identifying rock-forming minerals, the chemical properties are investigated by heating the specimen and also by adding hydrochloric acid to the sample. When the chemical composition of a substance is known, we can predict what will happen when an acid is added. Testing with a known sample and comparing it with an unknown sample gives us another clue to the identity of the unknown rock or mineral.

Minerals also have special physical properties unique to them. Magnetite is *magnetic.* Fluorite and certain types of calcite are *fluorescent* and glow with beautiful colors when they absorb energy from ultraviolet rays or X-rays and give off visible light. Pitchblende, which contains uranium, is *radioactive.* This invisible radiation can be detected by a Geiger counter. Another special physical property inherent in calcite crystals is that of *double refraction.* This means that when a beam of light is passed through the crystal, it is split into two beams. Also, if you look at an object through the crystal, you will see two images instead of one.

It is suggested that you have your students do the following practice activity before performing the specific tests. As you know, they may need to gain some skill in observing, describing, recording, distinguishing between physical and chemical properties, heating, and using acid. Be sure to have them use CAUTION when using hydrochloric acid (HCl). Remember hydrochloric acid is strong when diluted with water. If you have to dilute it yourself, place a pyrex container of water in a basin of water and slowly add acid. As an added precaution, place a glass rod in the pyrex container and run the acid slowly down it. The water in the basin will absorb some of the heat. If you do not have any HCl, use vinegar which is weak acetic acid.

Activity 1:   A PRACTICE INVESTIGATION FOR IDENTIFYING ROCK-FORMING MINERALS

MATERIALS (per student)

mineral-rock sample
magnifying glass
small pocket knife
penny
extra rock specimens
unglazed tile plates (streak plates)
chart or set of the 10 *Scale of Hardness* minerals

METHODS

Origin
1. Take your mineral-rock sample and examine it with your hand lens.
  a. Where did your rock come from?
  b. Is it a sedimentary, igneous or metamorphic rock in your opinion?
  c. What is your evidence for your answer to "b"?
Physical Properties
1. Take a closer look at your rock. Record the following in detail:
  a. Describe its shape.
  b. Measure its size.
  c. Weigh it. Would you say it is light or heavy for its size?
  d. What color is it?
  e. Does it have a luster or shine?

    f. Is it transparent, translucent or opaque?
2. Test for sound. Gently hit your sample on different surfaces. Describe the sound of your specimen.
3. Break off a piece of your rock if you can. Does your sample have an odor? Describe.
4. Put a piece of your rock to your tongue. Does it have a taste? Describe.
5. Simple test for hardness. Refer to the standard *Scale of Hardness* set.
    a. Try to scratch your rock with your fingernail. (Talc and gypsum can be scratched with a fingernail.)
    b. If you cannot scratch your rock with your fingernail, try scratching it with a penny. (Talc, gypsum and calcite can be scratched by a penny.)
    c. If the penny doesn't scratch the surface of your rock, use a pocket knife. (The blade will scratch talc, gypsum, calcite, fluorite and apatite.)
    d. Obtain another rock specimen and see if one will scratch the other. (Harder minerals can scratch softer ones and each mineral can scratch another of its kind.)
    e. What is the hardest mineral known? Is it listed on the *Scale of Hardness* chart?
6. Streak test.
    a. Obtain a piece of unglazed tile.
    b. Streak or try to make a mark on the tile with your rock.
    c. Does your rock make a streak or mark?
    d. What color is the streak?
7. Test for magnetism. Test your specimen with a magnet. Is it magnetic?
8. Test for radioactivity. Place a Geiger counter near your rock. Do you get a reading indicating that it is radioactive?
9. Test for fluorescence. Place your rock under an ultraviolet lamp. Is it fluorescent?
10. Test for double refraction. Shine an intense beam of light or a laser beam, if one is available, through your sample. Is the beam of light split into two beams? Look through the crystal at one object. Do you see two images?

Chemical Properties
1. Break off a piece of your rock sample and using tongs, hold the rock in the flame of a Bunsen burner or alcohol lamp.
    a. Does the rock change color?
    b. Does the rock melt?
    c. Does the rock burn?

2. Place a piece of rock in a pyrex beaker. Add a little acid very slowly.
   a. Does the acid cause bubbling? What do bubbles indicate is being formed?
   b. Describe the reaction as you see it.
   c. Express the reaction in words and try to write the equation for the reaction. For example, if your specimen is calcite, the chemical formula is $CaCO_3$.
   When hydrochloric acid is added to calcium carbonate, calcium chloride and water are formed and carbon dioxide bubbles off. This reaction is written as follows:

$$2HCl \quad + \quad CaCO_3 \longrightarrow CaCl_2 \quad + \quad H_2O \quad + \quad CO_2 \uparrow$$

| hydrochloric acid | + | calcium carbonate | yields calcium chloride | + | water | + | carbon dioxide gas |

Identification
1. What minerals have you found in your mineral-rock sample?
2. Do the results of your tests support your conclusions?

SHAPE: CRYSTAL FORM

BACKGROUND

Many rocks are amorphous in shape. However, the minerals within it may not be. When minerals occur in crystals the crystals are specific for that mineral and are sometimes easily identifiable. The typical hexagonal prisms of quartz are often enough to identify it. Crystals can be distorted, yet the angles between the prism faces will always be the same. For instance, in quartz, the angle between the faces is 60 degrees.

Sometimes twinning occurs. Staurolite, cerussite, and aragonite possess characteristic twin crystals.

Most rock-forming minerals are aggregates of imperfect crystal forms. Even though a specimen looks granular rather than crystalline, crystals can be seen under a microscope. Some crystals are elongated. Some look like columns such as can be seen in tourmaline. Others are flattened and look like blades as in kyanite and sibnite. Some are small and shaped like needles such as in pectolite and natrolite. Others are fibrous like in asbestos and some gypsum. Some radiate out from the center as can be seen in some pectolite and wavellite. Some minerals occur in crystalline plates or layers as is the case in mica. Other crystals are small and granular. Some can be seen with the naked eye and others can be viewed only under a microscope. In other cases, much depends on the location and conditions when the crystals are formed. As you probably know, stalactites are formed when water carrying minerals drip slowly in caves and form these unusual crystals.

So your students will become familiar with natural crystals and how crystals are formed, the following activities are suggested. Before you begin, collect reference books on rocks and minerals and pictures of crystals.

Activity 1: EXAMINING COMMON TABLE SALT (NaCl)

MATERIALS (per student)

NaCl crystals
stereoscopes or hand lenses
evaporating dishes or jar covers
water
toothpicks

METHODS

1. Place a pinch of salt under your stereoscope.
2. Move it around with a toothpick.
3. Draw, label and describe what you see.
4. What shape is the sodium chloride crystal?
5. How do you think the sodium and chlorine atoms are arranged in this structure?
6. Place some salt in an evaporating dish. Add water and mix with a toothpick until salt dissolves.
7. Leave in a warm place overnight.
8. Examine the salt water the next day. The water should have evaporated. Is there anything left?
9. What kind of rock formation have you started in your evaporating dish—sedimentary, igneous or metamorphic?

Activity 2: CRYSTALS IN ROCKS

MATERIALS (per student)

variety of rock specimens   probe

stereoscope or hand lenses forceps
styrofoam tray

METHODS

1. Take a rock sample, one at a time, and place it on your tray.
2. Examine it under the stereoscope.
3. Using your probe and forceps, loosen some crystals from your sample and observe.
4. Describe the shape of the crystals. Can you identify the structure? (There are six main crystal shapes: cubic, tetragonal, hexagonal, orthorhombic, monoclinic and triclinic.)

Activity 3: "GROWING" CRYSTALS

MATERIALS (per class)

6 quart jars per student
  hot plates
  Alum—$NaAl(SO_4)_2 \cdot 12H_2O$ or $KAl(SO_4)_2 \cdot 12H_2O$ (obtain from a pharmacy)
  water
  pans
  pencil per student
  string, cotton, pipe cleaners, etc.
  filter paper or paper towels
  funnels

METHODS

1. Fill jar with water to measure amount needed and pour into pan.
2. Bring water to a boil on hot plate or stove.
3. Add 3 oz. or about 90 ml of powdered alum to the boiling water. Let boil for a few more minutes and add a little more alum.
4. Filter alum solution into the jar while hot.
5. Place a pencil over the mouth of the jar and suspend from it a piece of string and a pipe cleaner. Drop a piece of cotton into the solution. These objects will provide places upon which the crystals will form.
6. Allow the solution to stand for 24 hours. While the solution is cooling, tap it occasionally then leave it undisturbed until the next day.

7. After two or three days, examine your alum crystals. What do you find?

8. Repeat the above with salt, sugar, borax, baking soda, Epsom salt, etc., so you will have a variety of crystals.

Note: When making solutions other than alum, add the crystal-forming substance to the cold water until no more dissolves, then heat to boiling and add more so you will have a saturated solution. The heating causes the molecules of water to move apart and therefore, more solute will dissolve in the solvent. When the solution cools, the excess will precipitate or fall out of solution. This is when crystallization begins. As the water evaporates, more crystals form and hence, the phrase, "growing" crystals.

CLEAVAGE AND FRACTURE

BACKGROUND

Cleavage refers to the tendency of minerals to break in definite directions which are always parallel to the crystal faces. The minerals split apart easily and the surfaces of the split are flat and smooth. These minerals split apart because they have zones of weakness. The weakness exists where the basic molecular structure of one molecule of the mineral joins another molecule. It is important for a gem stone cutter to be able to determine where these zones of weakness are. For example, if he is cutting a large diamond and miscalculates, the diamond will shatter into many pieces of lesser value than the cleanly cut two pieces he desired. Some minerals cleave only in one direction. Mica is one example and can be split into very thin sheets. Graphite and talc also have single cleavage. Other minerals cleave in two, three, or more directions. Feldspar cleaves in two directions: halite, galena and pyrite cleave in three directions.

Many minerals do not have zones of weakness and therefore do not cleave. When these minerals are broken, they *fracture* into pieces with rough, irregular surfaces. Quartz will fracture and so will obsidian.

So that your students will have a better idea of the meaning of cleavage and fracture, have them perform the following activity.

Activity 1:   EXAMINING CLEAVAGE AND FRACTURE

MATERIALS (per student or team of 2 or 3 students)

variety of crystalline rock specimens
variety of crystals grown in the laboratory

chisel or blunt knife
small hammer
stereoscopes or hand lenses
clay
styrofoam trays

METHODS

1. From your rock specimens, try to isolate some crystals.
2. Examine a crystal under the stereoscope and decide where you want to try to break it.
3. Place it on a piece of clay in your tray so it won't move around.
4. Place your chisel on the crystal and gently tap it with the hammer.
5. Were you successful in breaking it?
6. Did your specimen cleave or fracture?
7. Repeat the above steps using the laboratory grown crystals.

TENACITY

BACKGROUND

Tenacity refers to the resistance a mineral offers to breaking, cutting, bending or crushing. Most minerals are *brittle* and can be crushed to a fine power. A few are *malleable* and can be drawn out to a wire or hammered into plates. Soft minerals can be cut with a knife and are said to be *sectile*. Some minerals are *flexible* and are easily bent. Others are *elastic,* that is, they will spring back if stretched.

Activity 1: TESTING THE TENACITY OF MINERALS

MATERIALS (per student or team of 2 or 3 students)

variety of rock specimens
mortar and pestle
small hammer
pocket knife
pliers

METHODS

1. Isolate the minerals from the rock samples and perform the following tests on them.

2. Bend the mineral. Is it flexible?
3. Stretch the mineral. Is it elastic?
4. Pull on it with the pliers. Is it malleable?
5. Cut it with a knife. Is it sectile?
6. Crush it with a pestle in the mortar bowl. Is it brittle?
7. What can you conclude about each sample tested?

HARDNESS

BACKGROUND

Hardness should not be confused with tenacity. Tenacity is resistance to fracturing and cleaving. Yet a diamond, the hardest substance known, has a low tenacity because it cleaves readily. The hardness of a mineral is determined by how easily it scratches another mineral or how easily it is scratched. The German minerologist, Friedrich Mohs (1773-1839), devised a scale of hardness by arranging minerals in order according to their hardness from softest to hardest as follows:

#1 Talc, softest	#6 Feldspar
#2 Gypsum	#7 Quartz
#3 Calcite	#8 Topaz
#4 Fluorite	#9 Corundum
#5 Apatite	#10 Diamond, hardest

Moreover, hardness should not be confused with brittleness. A brittle mineral can be cracked and pulverized. A diamond is hard and brittle and will crack whereas a nail is hard but not brittle and will not crack when hit repeatedly with a hammer.

There is some correlation between hardness and the structure and chemical composition of minerals. Minerals of the heavy metals are soft (silver, copper, mercury and lead). Most sulfides, except those of iron, nickel and cobalt, are soft. Most hydrated (with water) minerals are soft. Minerals containing carbonate, sulfate and phosphates are relatively soft. Usually hard are the anhydrous (without water) oxides and silicates except for those of the heavy metals.

Activity 1:   THE HARDNESS TEST

MATERIALS (per student or team of 2 or 3 students)

a complete set of *Mohs' Scale of Hardness* minerals or a substitute set of the following items:

Item	*Hardness No.*
Fingernail	2 1/2
Copper penny	3
Knife blade	5
Window glass	5 1/2 - 6
Steel file	6 1/2 - 7

a set of minerals with unknown hardness numbers

METHODS

A. *Using Mohs' Scale of Hardness Minerals*
1. Scratch each unknown with the minerals in the Hardness set. Begin with the softest, talc, and proceed to the hardest, diamond.
2. When the known mineral scratches the unknown, reverse the procedure and see if the unknown scratches the known. Scratch the known below and above to be sure you have selected the right one.
3. Scratch it once more and be sure it is a true scratch and not just a chalk mark. Record this number for that particular sample.
4. Repeat the above with each unknown.

B. *Using the Substitute Hardness Set*
1. Scratch an unknown hardness mineral with each of the items in the hardness test set beginning with your fingernail.
2. Record the hardness number when you succeed in scratching your unknown mineral.
3. Repeat the above for each unknown.
4. From your results, can you make your own Hardness Scale of Minerals set with the unknown minerals you have in your collection?

LUSTER

BACKGROUND

Luster is the way a mineral reflects light or shines. Luster can be metallic or nonmetallic. A metallic shine is one that resembles highly polished metal such as gold, silver or aluminum. A nonmetallic luster is either dull or glassy. Minerals with a dull luster are bauxite and kaolin. Minerals with a glassy luster are feldspar, quartz and calcite.

Activity 1:   EXAMINING FOR LUSTER

MATERIALS (per class)

mineral samples
notebook

METHODS

1. Make two categories and four columns in your notebook and
   head them in this way:

Specimen	Metallic Luster	Nonmetallic Luster	
		Dull	Glassy

2. Examine each mineral specimen and record its luster under one
   of the columns above.

COLOR AND STREAK

BACKGROUND

   Color can be deceiving. Weathering can discolor minerals, and
therefore it is a good idea to scrape them to reveal the true color
underneath. Some minerals are also colored by impurities that obscure the true color of the mineral. If, when you streak the mineral on
an unglazed tile, it is the same color as the whole piece, the outer color
is not usually due to impurities. This streak test gives us clues to the
true color of the mineral. The streak is the true color of the mineral's
powder and contains very few impurities. If the mineral has a hardness greater than 6, it will not leave a streak on the streak plate.
Silicates usually have a white streak though some are gray or brown.
Other minerals which have characteristic streaks are sulfides, carbonates, oxides, phosphates, orsenates and sulfates of the heavier
metals.
   Some minerals have very definite colors and in these instances,
color can be used for identification. Sulfur is yellow, copper is
greenish-blue, vanadium is red, uranium is yellow, silicates with iron
in them are dark green to black, and silicates and carbonates with
manganese are pink.

Activity 1:   TESTING FOR TRUE COLOR

MATERIALS (per student)

mineral samples
pocket knife
porcelain streak plate or an unglazed tile

METHODS

1. Take one specimen at a time. What color is your sample?
2. Scrape some of the material off the surface of your mineral. Is it the same color? If it is, what does this mean? If it isn't, what does this indicate?
3. Scrape your mineral on the streak plate. Did it leave a mark? Is it the same color as your whole piece? What does this mean?
4. Repeat the same process with other specimens. What percent of your samples show their true colors?

DENSITY AND SPECIFIC GRAVITY

Density of a mineral is one of the best clues to its identity. *Density* is the weight or mass of a substance per unit volume. Related to density is *specific gravity* (S.G.). *S.G.* is the weight or mass of a substance compared to the weight or mass of an equal volume of water. Specific gravity gives us the ratio or tells us how much lighter or heavier a substance is compared to an equal volume of water.

The formula for specific gravity can be expressed thusly:

$$\text{S.G.} = \frac{\text{weight (mass) of substance (mineral)}}{\text{weight (mass) of equal volume of water}}$$

Let's take an example. Suppose we find that one cubic inch of galena weighs 32.5 ounces and one cubic inch of water weights 4.3 ounces. If we divide 32.5 by 4.3 we arrive at 7.55. This means that galena has a specific gravity of 7.55 or is 7.55 times heavier than water. Some substances such as ice or pine wood have S.G.'s less than 1 because they are lighter or less dense than water.

Since most rocks and minerals are not shaped in neat little cubes, there is another way to determine specific gravity by weighing the substance in air and then placing it in water. This method is illustrated for you and your students in the activity below.

Activity 1:   DETERMINING THE SPECIFIC GRAVITY OF MINERALS

MATERIALS (per student or team of 2 or 3 students)

spring scale
string
mineral specimens

METHODS

1. Attach the mineral you want to weigh.
2. Suspend it from the hook on the spring scale.
3. Record this weight. (#3_____)
4. Dip the specimen into the water so it is completely covered and record the weight. (The weight lost by the mineral in the water is the same as the weight of water it has displaced.) (#4_____)
5. Subtract #4 from #3 to get the weight lost in the water. (#5____)
6. Using this formula, find the specific gravity of the mineral:

$$\text{S.G.} = \frac{\text{weight (mass) of substance in air (\#3)}}{\text{weight (mass) lost by substance in water (\#5)}}$$

7. How does your substance compare in weight and density to water?

HEAT AND BURNING

BACKGROUND

Many minerals react in a predictable way when heated or burned. Some melt, others burst into flame and others are unaffected. Some elements produce brilliant colors when they are placed in a flame. Barium produces a yellow-green flame, for example. Other characteristic colors, produced by minerals are: boron—faint yellow-green, calcium—reddish-orange, copper—green, lithium—red, potassium—violet, sodium—yellow, and strontium—red.

Activity 1:   THE FLAME TEST FOR MINERALS

MATERIALS (per student or team of 2 or 3 students)

safety goggles

mineral specimens
long tongs or extra long forceps
Bunsen burner or alcohol lamp

METHODS

1. Put on goggles, and light your burner.
2. Take a small piece of your specimen with your tongs and place it in the flame. Answer the following questions:

   a. Does the mineral melt?
   b. Does it burn with a particular color?
   c. What is the color of the flame?
   d. Does it swell up, boil or violently disintegrate?
   e. What else do you observe?

3. If the fragment of specimen you heated in the flame gave off a characteristic color, what element or elements do you think are present?

TESTING WITH ACID

BACKGROUND

Hydrochloric acid (HCl) is used to further test for the identification of minerals. This is based on the solubility of the mineral in acid. The minerals with a metallic luster will react in one of three ways. Some are soluble, that is, they will dissolve in HCl. Some are soluble and produce chlorine, a greenish, poisonous gas. Others are soluble in HCl and form hydrogen sulfide (H_2S). H_2S can be recognized by its characteristic odor.

Minerals with a nonmetallic luster will react with HCl in four different ways. Some minerals are soluble in HCl, some are soluble and form silica gel, and some are decomposed by HCl leaving only a silica residue. All carbonates are soluble in HCl and give off bubbles of carbon dioxide (CO_2).

Activity 1:   THE ACID TEST

MATERIALS (per student or team of 2 or 3 students)

safety goggles
dilute (1:1) HCl

porcelain or pyrex container (beaker)
medicine dropper
mineral specimens

METHODS

1. Put on goggles. Place a small piece of your mineral specimen in a pyrex container (beaker). Does it have a metallic luster or not?
2. Add a few drops of HCl to the specimen. What happens? Is there any evidence of gas (bubbles)?
3. If there is a hood in the room, place your container and specimen under it. Otherwise, be sure there is good ventilation.
4. Cover the specimen with HCl.
5. Record your observations. Does it bubble? Does it have an odor? Does it dissolve?
6. Have you any idea what you have?

The study of determinative mineralogy is very complex and to try to highlight ways in which the amateur rock collector can identify rock-forming minerals is indeed a difficult task. It is strongly suggested that you urge your students to become serious students of chemistry if their interest in rocks and minerals persists, and that you seek more explicit information for identification in advanced books of minerology or in identification keys. Many young amateurs are content to identify their rock collections by comparing their samples with pictures in books.

KEY POINTS

Key Points and Activities

Be sure you know the meaning of the key terms in this chapter and practice using them.

mineral	saturated solution
rock	gem stone
igneous rock	cleavage
sedimentary rock	fracture
metamorphic rock	tenacity
physical property	brittle
chemical property	malleable
magnetism	sectile

fluorescence
radioactive
double refraction
Mohs' Scale of Hardness
crystal, crystallization
Hydrochloric Acid (HCl)
"Growing" crystals

flexible
elastic
luster
metallic, nonmetallic
Streak Plate Test for color
density, specific gravity
flame test for color
acid test for minerals

GLOSSARY

analogy — a resemblance to what is real or true; a substitute for, or model of, the real thing.

atmosphere — the air surrounding the earth.

chemical property — a characteristic way in which something reacts chemically with something else or combines to form a new product.

cleavage — the chemical bonding quality of a mineral that allows it to split apart into planes that always have the same angles in relation to each other.

crystal — refers to solids with regular geometric shapes and smooth flat surfaces that have been formed naturally. The flat surfaces are called crystal faces.

crystalline — refers to the orderly internal atomic arrangement of minerals.

fluorescence — having the ability to absorb invisible light rays and produce and emit light rays in the visible spectrum.

fracture — minerals lacking a symmetrical chemical bonding arrangement, and hence break apart into irregularly shaped parts.

hydrosphere — the water portion of the earth including ice.

lithosphere — the solid outer crust of the earth (*lithos* means stone).

luster — the way a mineral reflects light or shines.

magma — hot molten rock material from which igneous rocks are formed.

magnetic — attracted by a magnet.

mineral — an element or a mixture of chemical elements and/or chemical compounds. Some minerals consist of one element (graphite, carbon, gold); others of several elements or compounds (red iron ore, quartz, halite, calcite, feldspar).

physical property — a characteristic perceived through the senses; how something tastes, feels, smells, looks, sounds, etc.

rock — the solid form or building unit of the earth's crust; an aggregate of one or more substances, generally mineral.

tenacity — the resistance a mineral offers to breaking, cutting, bending or crushing.

ultraviolet rays — invisible rays with a wave length that is shorter than that of the violet rays in the visible spectrum.

X-rays — invisible rays of short wave length which are capable of passing through solid objects.

BIBLIOGRAPHY

Constant, Constantine, and Saul L. Geffner. *Earth Science Workbook*. New York: Amsco School Publications, Inc., 1972.

Earth Science Curriculum Project. *Investigating the Earth*. Boston: Houghton Mifflin Company, 1967.

Evans, Eva Knox. *The Question and Answer Book of Rocks*. New York: Golden Press, 1963.

Hyler, Nelson W. *The How and Why Wonder Book of Rocks and Minerals*. New York: Wonder Books, 1960.

Lemkin, William. *Visualized General Science*. New York: Oxford Book Company, 1964.

Lounsbury, John F., and Lawrence Ogden. *Earth Science*. New York: Harper & Row Publishers, 1969.

Mason, Brian, and L.G. Berry. *Elements of Mineralogy*. San Francisco: W.H. Freeman and Company, 1968.

Shelton, John S. *Geology Illustrated*. San Francisco: W. H. Freeman and Company, 1966.

Weaver, Jay D., and Charles T. Wolf. *Modern Mathematics for Elementary Teachers*. 2nd edition. Scranton, Pennsylvania: International Textbook Company, 1968.

Weisbruch, Fred T., et al. *Patterns and Processes of Science, Laboratory Text No. 3*. Boston, Massachusetts: D.C. Heath and Company, 1968.

9

Guidelines for Soil Studies

IDENTIFYING SOIL TEXTURES AS SAND, SILT, AND CLAY

BACKGROUND

The texture of the soil refers to the size of the particles in the soil and to the relative proportions of sand, silt, and clay. The sizes of the particles in sand range from 1/500—1/25 inch or .005—1 mm in diameter; in silt from 1/5000—1/500 inch or .0005—.005 mm; and in clay under 1/5000 inch or .0005 mm in diameter. Some authorities consider a fourth textural category, that of gravel with particles over 1/25 inch or 1 mm in diameter. The term soil, however, is used only for compositions having less than 90% gravel. When classifying soils according to texture, one first determines the gravel content, then the proportions of sand, silt, and clay.

Activity 1: EXAMINING SOIL AND SOIL PARTICLES

MATERIALS (per team of 2 or 3 students)

trowel	large plastic bags
garden spade	set of fine mesh sieves
glass jars for soil	newspaper

METHODS

1. Collect soil samples from different areas and place them in plastic bags to carry back to school. Then display them in the glass jars. Record date of collection and location.

2. Collect different soil samples with apparent different characteristics. Carry them back to school in plastic bags. Record the date and the location of each sample. Use these samples for the tests that follow.

3. Take a measured (by volume) amount of each soil sample and sift it through the sieves using the largest mesh sieve first and finish with the smallest mesh sieve. Collect the sifted soil on newspaper and pour each fraction into a glass jar. Label.

4. Repeat the above until the whole sample has been sifted and separated into fractions.

5. Estimate the proportion of the soil that can be categorized as gravel, sand, silt, and clay.

6. Examine each fraction under the stereoscope or view with a hand lens. Describe. Can you recognize the minerals present?

7. Test further for sand, silt, and clay. Add water to each fraction and roll it to see if it sticks together or crumbles.

Clay will stick together. Feels sticky when wet.
Sand crumbles and falls apart. Feels gritty.
Silt is somewhere in between. Feels like talcum powder or flour.

8. Repeat the above with many of your soil samples. When you finish your work, save the fractions from four of your soil samples. With one sample, layer a fraction over another in a glass jar to produce a soil profile for display. With another sample, save each jar as examples of soil variation and label them gravel, sand, silt, and clay. Put aside the other two soil samples for studies described later on.

Activity 2:   DETERMINING WHICH SOIL IS BEST FOR GROWING PLANTS

MATERIALS (per team of 2 or 3 students)

soil fractions (gravel, sand, silt and clay saved from Activity 1)
paper cups or styrofoam cups or coffee cans lined with waxed paper
  or flower pots
lima been seeds, radishes, corn or others of your choice
aluminum pie plates or saucers

METHODS

1. If you do not use flower pots, punch a hole in your containers. Label four containers: SAND, SILT, CLAY, MIXTURE.

2. Place a layer of gravel on the bottom of each flower pot. Layer sand over the gravel in one, silt over another, clay over the third and put equal amounts of each in the last container.

3. In each pot, plant two seeds each of limas, radishes and corn. Give equal amount of water every other day. Place in a warm sunny place.

4. Observe your seeds growing each day and record each day's observations, the amount of water used and when watered, on a chart that should be left with the flower pot.

5. As the seeds germinate and the plants grow, record their heights. Plot them on a piece of graph paper and construct a histogram (bar graph) to show the relative heights of the plants. Use colored pencil to differentiate the limas from the radishes and the corn plants.

6. Compare your graphs. How are they the same? How are they different?

7. Compare and contrast the growth of the beans in each pot, the radishes and the corn plants.

8. Try to answer the following questions:
   a. Which seeds sprouted first? In which soil?
   b. In which soil do they grow fastest?
   c. After a few weeks, which plants appear to be healthiest? In which soil?

9. What conclusions can you draw from the results of your experiment?

10. As an extension of this experiment, vary the amounts of the different types of soil and compare the growth. When you have experimented enough to recommend a particular mixture and proportions of each fraction or type of soil, then add varying amounts of chemicals such as phosphorous, nitrogen and potassium compounds, or fertilizers, to see if you can improve upon your soil mixture.

ILLUSTRATING HOW FAST SOIL WILL ABSORB WATER

BACKGROUND

In determining the way land may be used, it is important to determine and know the *percolation rate* of the area, that is, the rate at which the soil will absorb water. Obviously the more porous the soil is, the more water can be absorbed. Sand is of a large particle size and the spaces between the granules are large. This means that water will be absorbed rapidly and sink well below the surface. Silt will not absorb the water as rapidly and clay will not absorb water very quickly at all because clay has very small pore spaces. Anticipated results, however, do not depend upon porosity alone. The ground cover plays an important role in determining how fast water will be absorbed. For instance, if the ground is barren, rain water hits the soil and spatters, whereas if there is a ground cover, the water hits the plants and slowly seeps to the ground and into the soil. The reason for this is that the rain hitting the ground directly actually causes the large pores to become closed whereas the indirect raindrops do not and the water is absorbed quickly. Another factor to be considered is that soil is not just clay or silt or sand but rather a mixture. This means that there are small and large holes in the soil, or to say it another way, there are varying sized pores. When water flows into the smaller pores, it has a tendency, because of its adhesive, cohesive and capillary properties, to cling to the soil and eventually rise to the surface.

Activity 1:   MEASURING THE RATE AT WHICH SOIL ABSORBS WATER(PERCOLATION TEST)

MATERIALS (per team of 2 or 3 students)

2 lb. or .906 kg. coffee can or a 40 oz. or 1.183 liters juice can
ruler   board
masking tape   hammer

METHODS

1. Remove the lid from a large can. Measure up 2 inches or 5 cm from the open end and mark it.
2. Remove the lid from the other end of the can. Place a board on the top of the can and drive it 2 inches or 5 cm into the ground.
3. Place the ruler inside the can so it touches the ground. Tape it in place.
4. Fill the can with water up to the 7 inch or 17.8 cm mark on the ruler.
5. Using a sweep second watch or a stop-watch, record the time it takes for the water to go down each inch interval. Record.
6. Select another area of soil and repeat the above. Try to select areas where the soil texture varies and compare results. Which soils absorb water fastest? Slowest?

Activity 2:   MEASURING THE RATE AT WHICH FOUR TYPES OF "SOIL" ALLOW WATER TO PASS THROUGH

MATERIALS (per team of 2 or 3 students)

18 in. or 45.8 cm plastic column with mesh screen, tube and pinch
   clamp on bottom
stand and clamp to hold the column in place
soil fractions (gravel, sand, silt and clay from Activity 1 in the first
   section of this chapter)
250 ml graduated cylinder
400 or 500 ml beaker or collection jar

METHODS

1. Measure out 100 ml of gravel and place in the column. Be sure
   the pinch clamp is closed.
2. Pour a measured amount of water into the column that just
   covers the gravel. Record the volume of water needed to cover
   the particles. Calculate the percentage of space between the
   particles (porosity).

   Suppose 50 ml water was needed to cover the 100 ml of gravel.

   $$\frac{50 \text{ ml water}}{100 \text{ ml particles}} = \frac{1}{2} \text{ or 50\% space}$$

3. Open the clamp and let the water drain into the beaker. Measure
   the amount that came through the gravel and subtract it from
   the 50 ml added.

   Suppose 35 ml came through.
   50 ml - 35 ml = 15 ml*

4. Now add 300 ml of water to the column, and time how fast the
   water runs through into the beaker. This will give you the
   permeability of the gravel and the rate at which water can pass
   through particles the size of gravel.
5. Repeat the above using sand, silt, and clay.

-----

*Note: The amount of water left in the soil is called *capillary water*. This water is
retained in the soil by surface tension and by the attraction of the water molecules to
the solid soil particles.
   Capillary water can only be removed by evaporation into the air or by absorption
into the root systems of plants. It cannot be removed by gravity.

6. Graph the results and compare the permeability and porosity of each soil type.
7. Why would this information be important to land and water planning agencies for assessing the capability of a soil to transmit effluent from on-site sewage systems or to estimate the rate of movement of leachate from sanitary landfill areas?

PRACTICAL WAYS TO MEASURE THE WATER CONTENT OF THE SOIL

BACKGROUND

Water content of the soil is the amount of water in the soil at any given time. Previous experiments have revealed that some soils can hold more water than others so it is reasonable to predict that you and your students may find varying amounts of water in a measured amount of soil taken from different locations on a given day.

The capacity of soils to retain and store water varies considerably according to several factors. Less water clings to sand because the particles are large and have less surface area than do smaller particles. The pores are large and the water runs right through sandy soil. Sandy soil may store only 10 to 15 per cent of its weight. Finer textured soils have smaller particles and smaller pores which hold back the water and discharge it slowly. Clay may store as much as 50 to 70 per cent of its weight because the particles are very fine and water adheres readily to them. The water retention capacity increases with increased amounts of humus or organic matter. Soils with humus may retain as much as 100 to 200 percent of its own weight in water. Humus will hold water for two days after a rainstorm and discharge it slowly into the surrounding area. In fact, about 0.8 inches or 2 cm of water is stored for each one inch or 2.5 cm of humus.

Activity 1:   TO DETECT THE WATER CONTENT OF SOIL

MATERIALS (per team of 2 or 3 students)

3 pyrex dishes or 3 crucibles
3 watch glasses to fit over the crucibles
   Bunsen burner, or alcohol lamp, or propane burner, or hot plate

METHODS

2. Cover each pyrex dish with another one or cover each crucible with a watch glass.

3. Heat the soil samples gently. Do you see evidence of water collecting on the surface of the tops?

Activity 2: TO DETERMINE THE AMOUNT OF WATER IN A SOIL SAMPLE

MATERIALS (per team of 2 or 3 students)

small can
small filter paper or paper toweling cut to the diameter of the can
drying oven or heat lamp
balance

METHODS

1. Punch several holes in the bottom of the can to accelerate the drying process.
2. Fit a piece of filter paper on the bottom of the can so the soil won't fall out.
3. Weigh the can and the filter paper. Record _____
4. Weigh out 50 grams of your soil sample and place it in the can. Weigh the can and its contents. Record _____
5. Place the can in a drying oven at 105° F or 40° C for 24 to 48 hours to dry, or leave under a heat lamp or on a radiator to drive off the moisture for 3 to 5 days.
6. When you are reasonably sure all the water has been driven off, place a watch glass on the top of the can for a day or so and check to see if any water collects on the glass.
7. When the soil sample is dry, remove from the heat and allow to cool thoroughly.
8. Weigh the can and the contents after drying and cooling. Record _____.
9. Subtract the amount in #8 from #4 above and record _____. This will give you the weight of the water since the difference is attributed to the water loss.
10. Now subtract the weight of the can and filter recorded in #3 above from the weight of the can and contents after drying, #8. This will give you the weight of the dried soil. Record _____.
11. Calculate the water content using the following formula:

$$\% \text{ Water Content} = \frac{\text{Loss in weight of soil (#9)}}{\text{Dry weight of soil (#10)}} \times 100$$

EASY WAYS TO FIND THE WATER HOLDING CAPACITY OF THE SOIL

BACKGROUND

Soils which readily become saturated with water are usually located above an impermeable soil layer or bedrock. Generally, these conditions prevail in flat areas where the water table fluctuates through a narrow range. If soils in a particular locality remain saturated, this would be no place to bury solid wastes or to install septic tanks. The waste would become dangerous leachate. In order for waste material to purify naturally, it must filter slowly through the soil. This would be impossible if the soil were normally filled with water. The liquid waste would flow faster than the soil could absorb it and would soon rise to the surface and contaminate the area.

In the last section, your students studied how fast the soil could fill with water and how fast water could drain through different types of soil. In this section they will learn how to determine the water holding capacity of the soil or how much water soil is capable of holding. We have already learned that soils containing much humus will hold great amounts of water and will retain it for a long time. The students will now have an opportunity to test this.

Activity 1: DETERMINING THE WATER HOLDING CAPACITY OF SOIL

MATERIALS (per team of 2 or 3 students)

dried soil sample from Activity 2 in previous section
cloth to cover can
tape
pail or container larger than soil can
can opener
wire or twine

METHODS

1. Weigh your soil sample and can again. Record _____ .
2. Using a can opener, make two holes at the top of the open end of your soil sample can and attach a wire or a piece of twine through them so that the can can be suspended later on in the experiment.

3. Submerge the can in a pail of water overnight to saturate the soil sample.
4. The next day, remove the can from the water and hang it up to drain for 30 minutes.
5. Wipe off the outside of the can and weigh it. Record_____.
6. Subtract #1 above from #5. The difference is the weight of the water the soil absorbed. Record _____.
7. Calculate the water holding capacity using the following formula:

$$\% \text{ Water Holding Capacity} \quad = \quad \frac{\text{Gain in weight (\#6)}}{\text{Dry weight (\#1)}} \quad X \quad 100$$

Activity 2: COMPARING THE WATER HOLDING CAPACITY OF SOIL TYPES

MATERIALS (per team of 2 or 3 students)

samples of different soil types saved from Activity 1 in the first section of this chapter
drying oven or heat lamp
4 aluminum pans
4 glass jars of equal volume with tops
250 ml graduated cylinder

METHODS

1. Pour gravel from your soil samples into an aluminum pan. Pour the sand into another, silt into a third and clay into a fourth pan.
2. Place the pans in a drying oven at 105° F or 40° C for 24 to 48 hours or place under a heat lamp or on a radiator.
3. To test for the presence of moisture, transfer a scoopula of each soil onto a dry piece of cobalt chloride ($CoCl_2$) paper. If the soil is dry the cobalt chloride paper will stay blue. If the soil still has moisture in it, the paper will turn pink.
4. Weigh out exactly 100 grams of each soil fraction and place in the glass jars. Label the jars GRAVEL, SAND, SILT, CLAY.
5. Add a measured amount of water to each of the soil samples keeping track of the exact amount you have added. Add as much as the soil can hold, that is, to the point where it appears the soil can hold no more water. Record this amount on a card and the time you added the water. Leave the card with the sample.

6. Shake each sample vigorously 25 times and let the soil settle for 30 minutes. Has more water been absorbed or can you see water on the surface?

7. If more water appears to have been absorbed, add another measured amount to the point where it appears the soil can absorb no more water. Record this amount and the time on your card. Shake again as before and let settle for 30 minutes.

8. If the samples in #6 have water on their surfaces, do not add more water, but rather, shake another 25 times and let settle for another 30 minutes.

9. Repeat the above procedures until all the samples remain with some water on the surface. Compare the amount of water you had to add in order to collect water on the surface.

Gravel_____ml water added
Sand _____ml water added
Silt _____ml water added
Clay_____ml water added

Which fraction absorbed the most water?
Which fraction absorbed the least?
What are some of the causes of these differences?

10. Punch a hole in the top of each jar, invert it and suspend it in some way so the water can drain out of the jar. Do one sample at a time and time the rate of flow. Place a collecting jar under the sample to catch the water. Repeat the procedure with the other samples.

11. Pour the drain water into a graduated cylinder and record the amount on the proper card. Do the same with the other drain water. Compare the amounts of water drained through each sample.

Gravel _____ml drain water
Sand _____ml drain water
Silt_____ml drain water
Clay_____ml drain water

Which fraction allowed more water to drain through it?
Which fraction retained more water?
What are some of the causes of these observations?

12. Go out-of-doors and get different samples of soil. Obtain samples devoid of vegetation, and samples with much organic material. Repeat the above experiment. Which soils have the best water holding capacities?

Activity 3:   SIMULATION GAME—LAND AND WATER PLANNING

MATERIALS (per class)

information on local government

information on regional planning for land and water use (obtain from your State Office of State Planning)

topographical maps of your area (obtained from the town hall or from the U.S. Geological Survey office in your area)

information on local building codes (obtained from town hall)

METHODS

1. Form the following groups and randomly assign students to play individual roles in the game.

State Committees:
  Geology professor—Mr. Joseph
  U.S. Geological Survey—Mr. Frederick
  U.S. Geological Survey—Mr. Raymond
  State Agricultural Experiment Station—Dr. Alice
  State Sanitary Engineer—Mr. Allen
Town Committee:
  Town Health Officer—Dr. Patrick
  Town Planning and Zoning, Chairman—Mr. Robert
  Town Sanitary Engineer—Mr. Herman
  Town Manager (Mayor, First Selectman)—Mr. Herbert
  Town Conservation Commission, Chairman—Mr. Phillip
Citizens Groups:
  Residents Pro Sanitary Landfill, Chairman—Mr. Guy
  Residents Con Sanitary Landfill, Chairman—Mr. William
Pressure Groups:
  Citizens for a Quality Environment, Chairman—Mrs. Helen

Note: You may add roles for more students to play or give each player an assistant or assign students to subcommittees.

2. *The Problem.* A regional planning group, consisting of your town and three adjoining towns, is contemplating locating a sanitary landfill in your town. They are investigating a site close to a swamp and on the border of a residential area. The town at present owns the land. The residents in the locality are against it while the residents on the other end of town think it is fine

because they have to pay to have their garbage trucked out of town. The Environmental group is afraid it will contaminate the area and destroy the swamp. Thus far the State Committee has collected the data below:

The soil in the area is saturated with water within 3 feet or .912 meter of the surface less than 2 months of the year.
There is a temporary high water table within 3 feet or .912 meter of the surface.
The water table fluctuates over a wide range and in the spring, the water may be only 15 to 20 inches or 37.7 to 50.9 cm. below the surface.
It is classified as an imperfectly drained area, because in the spring the amount of leachate will be greater following long periods of rain. This may affect the quality of the ground-water and surface-water.
The Committee recommends that *if* the land is to be used for sanitary landfill, it must be drained or the leachate should be controlled in some way.

The towns, with the help of the government officials and the citizens, will have to decide whether or not the sanitary landfill should be located on this site.

3. Examine local topographic maps of your area and see if you can locate a site similar to the one described above. If so, the game will be more meaningful if students can relate it to something familiar. If there is no such area, let them use their imaginations and create it and draw their own map.

4. Tell the students they are to play the roles to which they have been assigned. Have them do some background reading and to contact local groups similar to the ones in the game. Make the game as authentic as possible.

5. Each member of each group must prepare a case to present at an open hearing. Have them elect their own moderator and establish their own rules.

FACTORS DETERMINING THE WAY LAND SHOULD BE USED

BACKGROUND

If you look through the chapters on land, you can pick out some of the factors which should be considered when determining the way land should be used. Discuss these factors with your students. Ask some basic questions: Where is the land located? Is it sloped or flat? What is the covering vegetation? What natural resources are evident? What is the composition and profile of the land? What rock formations can be seen? What is the texture of the soil? What is the percolation rate and the water holding capacity of the soil? What natural and man-made objects surround the land? How can it be used and conserved at the same time?

In the United States, 58% of the land is used for raising livestock and growing crops. More than 22% is ungrazed forest. Less than 3% is urbanized and is used for transportation. Open space areas such as parks, wildlife refuges, public installations and recreation areas account for about 5% of the land and the remaining 12% is limited use land—tundra, desert, swamp and so on. We have grown up with the idea that land is a limitless commodity yet, most of the wilderness is gone and we have learned that land, in reality, is a finite environmental community. Local governments have the primary authority over land use. It is everyone's responsibility however, to work with the town officials on common goals and to plan carefully for the future.

Presently, there are about 11 acres of land for each person in the United States. This is one-third what it was at the beginning of the century. It is estimated that there will be only 7 acres or 2.828 hectares of land per person by 2000. Although in recent years Congress has appropriated funds to purchase 4 million acres for the national park system, it appears to be not nearly enough.

There are many facets to this problem; therefore, in order to have your students investigate this aspect in depth, urge them to collect and read related resource materials. Several types of documents are available from State and Federal Agencies by writing to the agency directly or writing to your Senator or Congressman in Washington, D.C. Usually, if you only ask for one copy, your representative will send you what you request free of charge. Activity 1 below relates to collecting these documents.

Activity 1:   COLLECTING OFFICIAL DOCUMENTS TO ASSIST IN DETERMINING THE WAY LAND SHOULD BE USED

MATERIALS (per class)

1. *Topographic Maps*—compiled by the U.S. Geological Survey (U.S. Department of the Interior)—shows the configuration of the land surface. (Tell them which area you want.)
2. *Bedrock-Geology Maps*—U.S. Geological Survey, Geologic Division—shows an interpretation of the near-surface distribution of bedrock as determined by the known outcrops.

3. *Surficial-Geology Maps*—U.S. Geological Survey, Geologic Division—shows the distribution of unconsolidated material of varying thickness layered between the soil layer and bedrock. Also designate areas that have been filled for such man-made projects as highways, solid-waste storage, sanitary landfill, and flood control.

4. *Soil-Survey Maps*—U.S. Soil Conservation Service in cooperation with the Department of Agriculture in your state— indicate the properties a soil scientist uses to delineate each area: (1) Properties of the soil itself, such as color, texture, structure, structural arrangement and depth of layers (horizons), temperature, permeability, pH, drainage, and organic matter content; (2) they also include reference to the description of the landscape on which the soil is placed such as slope, amount of exposed bedrock, surface stoniness, erosion, and possibility of flooding.

5. *Water-Resource Inventories*—U.S. Geological Survey Water Resource Division—identify and discuss the quantity and quality of water available within the state. Include detailed information on the surface water from lakes, ponds and streams, showing amounts of usable storage, high and low flow frequency and duration, frequency of floods, and storage required to maintain various flows. Data available for ground water include well records, pumping-test data, ground-water level measurements and stream-flow records.

6. *Land Use and Zoning Inventories*—available from the State Planning Agency or the local Planning and Zoning Commission—show areas in the state and local community used for residential, commercial, industrial, transportation, cultural, entertainment, and recreation, communications and utilities, resource production and extraction, open and forested spaces, and wetlands.

METHODS

1. Have your students write to your Senator or Congressman or directly to the agencies above and ask for the appropriate documents for *your state and locality.*

2. While you are waiting for the documents to arrive, have the students familiarize themselves with the regulations pertaining to land, water, and natural resources in your own community. Inasmuch as land, water and mineral resources vary from one section of the country to another, the usual practice is for Zoning

and Planning regulations to be devised and enforced at the local level.

3. When the documents arrive, have the students study them, keeping in mind what your local regulations are in determining how land should be used. Do the students agree for the most part with the local authorities or not? Can they support their positions?

Activity 2:   PLANNING YOUR OWN COMMUNITY

MATERIALS

The same as in Activity 1 above.

METHODS

1. Locate your town on a map.
2. Pretend that your town is undeveloped land and your class has the responsibility of planning it. Set up planning and development committees and subcommittees to advise your Town Manager as he or she plans the town.

   What committees should be organized? What State and Federal Agencies might be consulted? What organizations might need to be hired?

Local Planning and Zoning Commission
Town Engineer
Town Conservation Commission
Town Sanitation Engineer
Board of Education
Chamber of Commerce
Transportation Commission
Building Inspector
Sanitation Engineer
Water Commission
Sewer Commission
Representatives from the utility companies (electric, gas, telephone)
Parks and Recreation
Board of Realtors
The Private Architect and Land Design Corporation
The Private Land Development Corporation
The Private Land Planning Consultants (Civil Engineers)
Cultural and Entertainment Committee
Public Health Committee

Senior Citizens Committee
Public Safety Committee (Police and Fire)

3. Have the students in the class select the committee on which they wish to work.
4. Let the students elect their own Town Manager to direct the planning operation. You, as the teacher, act as an outside Organization and Planning Consultant and guide them in their studies.

KEY POINTS

Key Points and Activities

Soil texture is determined by particle size:

gravel—over 1/25 inch or 1 mm.
sand—1/500—1/25 inch or .005—1 mm.
silt—1/5000—1/500 inch or .0005—.005 mm.
clay—under 1/5000 inch or .0005 mm.

Soils with large particles will absorb water faster than soils with small particles.
The more humus, or organic matter, present in the soil, the more water will be absorbed and stored.
The water holding capacity is basically determined by the spaces between the particles of soil.
Community planning must be a community project. Have your class make a study of your local community and determine to what degree the residents are in fact involved in town planning.

GLOSSARY

adhesion — ability of water molecules to cling to other surfaces.
capillary water — tiny droplets of water that are held by adhesion and cohesion in the upper few feet of soil. This water provides the water supply for plants between rainfalls.
cohesion — ability of water molecules to cling together.
permeability —rate at which water can pass through a porous material.
porosity — the percentage of space between the grains of soil. The porosity of a soil influences its permeability.
water content — the amount of water in the soil at any given time.
water holding capacity — the amount of water a soil can hold when saturated.

BIBLIOGRAPHY

Hone, Elizabeth B., Alexander Joseph, and Edward Victor. *A Sourcebook for Elementary Science.* New York: Harcourt, Brace & World, Inc., 1962.

Joseph, Alexander et al. *A Sourcebook for the Physical Sciences.* New York: Harcourt, Brace & World Inc., 1961.

Laun, H. Charles. *The Natural History Guide.* Alton, Illinois: Alsace Books and Films, 1970.

Lounsbury, John F., and Lawrence Ogden. *Earth Science.* New York: Harper & Row, 1969.

Pettit, Ted S. *A Guide to Nature Projects.* New York: W.W. Norton & Company, 1966.

Thurber, Walter A., and Robert E. Kilburn. *Exploring Earth Science.* Boston: Allyn and Bacon, Inc. 1970.

U.N.E.S.C.O. *700 Science Experiments for Everyone.* Garden City, New York: Doubleday & Company, Inc., 1958.

10

Studying Interaction
Among Living Things

INVESTIGATING HOW PLANTS AND ANIMALS INTERACT WITH THEIR ENVIRONMENT AND WITH EACH OTHER

BACKGROUND

In this chapter, your students should be able to see the significance of interaction among living things. Begin by having them ask and try to answer some basic questions.

Look around you. Are you alone? Are there other people with you? Can you see other animals or plants from where you are? Do you think that the things you can see have an effect on you or each other? Of course, they do! All living things have an influence on one another. You are not the same as you were a while ago. You are always changing as a result of what is going on around you and inside you. All your surroundings have an effect on you.

Animals, including man, and plants are living and have similar needs. Living things need water, need to eat, need to breathe and need to produce new generations of baby plants and animals. If living things did not reproduce, individual plants and animals would disappear from the planet earth.

Water is found in all living things. Some living things, however, need more water than other living things. When animals eat plants and other animals, they take in water and nourishment in order to stay alive. When animals and plants die, they decay and return water and minerals to the ground. The plants take in the water and minerals from the soil and use them to grow.

Ask the students to take a deep breath. The air you just took into your lungs contains 21% oxygen gas. Oxygen is needed to break down food. The oxygen combines with the food and is changed to carbon dioxide, water and energy. This is a chemical process called *respiration*. This change can be written chemically and the following is called a *chemical reaction:*

oxygen	+	food	yields	carbon dioxide	+	water	Energy
$6O_{2(g)}$	+	$C_6H_{12}O_{6(s)}$	$\longrightarrow$	$6CO_{2(g)}$	+	$6H_2O_{(l)}$	+	E

The mechanical way in which a living thing takes in oxygen and gives off carbon dioxide is called *breathing*. For example, man breathes with lungs. A fish breathes by means of gills. All living things carry on respiration but they do not all breathe in the same way.

Ask your students if plants breathe? Do they use oxygen and form carbon dioxide? Certainly. A plant is living and must use oxygen to break down starch to sugar in order to use the food it has made. Where does the supply of oxygen come from? From the plants themselves. Although plants use oxygen during respiration, they also give off oxygen when they are making food.

In order to make food, plants must have the green pigment, chlorophyll, in their leaves. They also need a source of energy. Where does the energy come from? All energy comes from the sun. The plant has the ability to take carbon dioxide and water, with the help of chlorophyll and light energy, and change it to food and oxygen gas.

This way of making food by green plants is called *photosynthesis*. Photosynthesis can be written chemically also. The reaction looks like this:

carbon dioxide	+	water	yields light energy chlorophyll	sugar	+	oxygen
$6CO_{2(g)}$	+	$6H_2O_{(l)}$	$\xrightarrow[\text{chlorophyl}]{\text{light energy}}$	$C_6H_{12}O_{6(s)}$	+	$6O_{2(g)}$

Where does the carbon dioxide come from so that the plant can use it? Carbon dioxide comes mainly from animals. What would happen if all the plants on the earth suddenly died? Have the students discuss this and study the reactions for photosynthesis and respiration.

Respiration

oxygen	+	food	yields	carbon dioxide	+	water	
$6O_{2(g)}$	+	$C_6H_{12}O_{6(s)}$	$\longrightarrow$	$6CO_{2(g)}$	+	$6H_2O_{(l)}$	Energy

Photosynthesis

carbon dioxide	+	water	yields light energy chlorophyl	sugar	+	oxygen
$6CO_{2(g)}$	+	$6H_2O_{(l)}$	$\xrightarrow[\text{chlorophyl}]{\text{light energy}}$	$C_6H_{12}O_{6(s)}$	+	$6O_{2(g)}$

All living things are able to have babies that look like them. Have you ever seen a dog give birth to kittens? Dogs have *puppies* and *cats* have kittens! When the puppies grow up, they have more pups, and when the kittens grow up, they have more kittens and so it is with all other living things.

Plants grow up, produce flowers and the flowers form seeds. When the seeds fall to the ground, they grow into new plants. What would happen if there were only three maple trees left in the world and you collected all the seeds? What role does man play in the way plants and animals interact with one another? Pose these questions to your students before going on.

Activity 1:   EXAMINING THE REACTION FOR RESPIRATION AND PHOTOSYNTHESIS

MATERIALS (per student)

paper and pencil

METHODS

1. Write the chemical reaction for respiration in words.
2. Write the reaction for respiration by using formulas and balance the equation.
3. Write the chemical reaction for photosynthesis in words.
4. Write the reaction for photosynthesis by using formulas and balance the equation.
5. What do you notice about the reactions?
6. Can you think of a way to combine the reactions? If so, rewrite both reactions as one equation.
7. Define respiration.
8. Define photosynthesis.

STUDYING HOW ANIMALS AND PLANTS INTERACT FOR WATER AND FOOD

Water is needed to dissolve minerals in the soil. Plants take in the water and minerals through tiny *root hairs* on their roots. The water enters the root hairs and moves from cell to cell. The water keeps the plant rigid. The water also carries minerals and gases throughout the plant and is important in photosynthesis. (Figure 10-1.)

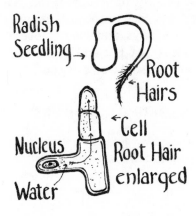

Radish
Seedling→

Root
Hairs

Cell

Nucleus

Root Hair
enlarged

Water

Figure 10-1.

When a plant has more water than it can use, it gets rid of it by the process of transpiration. The plant has small pores called *stomates*. The stomates are located primarily on the underside of the leaf, and there are two cells around each stomate called *guard cells*. The guard cells relax and allow the water out. When the plant needs water, the guard cells close the stomates, keeping the plant from drying out. (Figure 10-2.)

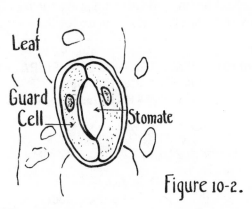

Leaf

Guard
Cell

Stomate

Figure 10-2.

Animals need water in the air in order to keep their mouths, noses and lungs moist. Animals also drink water and eat foods that have water in them so that their bodies won't dry out. About 80% of the body is water. Some animals, like the fish, must stay in the water all the time, while other animals live part of their lives in the water and the other part on land. The frog is one such animal.

As a tadpole, the frog lives in the water, and as an adult, the frog lives on land; however, it doesn't stray too far from the water. The frog must keep its skin moist so that it can breathe through it when it is resting. It can also breathe through its mouth if it doesn't jump around too much. The frog also has lungs, and when it is very active, it uses its lungs to breathe. When it is very hot and dry in the summer, the frog will bury itself in the wet mud so it won't dry out.

Activity 1:   INVESTIGATING ROOT HAIRS

MATERIALS (per team of 2 or 3 students)

radish seeds
paper towel
jar or beaker

METHODS

1. Place some radish seeds in a paper towel.
2. Moisten the towel and place in a jar or beaker.
3. Let stand for a few days where they won't dry out.
4. Examine the fuzzy root and root hairs under a magnifying lens or microscope. The tiny hairlike things are the *root hairs*.
5. Try to figure out what the root hairs do for the plant.

Activity 2:   INVESTIGATING TRANSPIRATION
(loss of water through
the pores in the leaf)

MATERIALS (per class or team of 2 or 3 students)

potted plant or
growing plant, shrub or tree branch outdoors
plastic bag and tie

METHODS

1. Find a branch or entire small plant with many leaves on it.
2. Place plastic bag over branch or plant and seal the end with the tie.
3. If you are carrying out this investigation outdoors in warm

weather you may use the next 20—30 minutes to observe the area for evidence of interaction, etc. and then return to your plant. If you are using a plant in the classroom, observations may be made the following day.

4. Observe your branch or plant.
5. What do you observe about the inside of the plastic bag?
6. What do you think caused this?
7. What has happened to the leaves of the plant or shrub?

Can you figure out what might happen if there were *acid* in the air instead of water? When animals *respire,* water is formed. Some of the water stays in the animal's body and the rest is given off as waste. Man gets rid of liquid waste as urine, as *perspiration* and as water droplets when he *exhales.* Ask the students what happens when they blow their breath on a cold window pane.

Activity 3:   INVESTIGATING RATE OF TRANSPIRATION

MATERIALS

green plant   stand with 2 clamps
rubber or plastic hose   glass or glass chimney
glass tube or straw

METHODS

1. Find a stem of a plant with many leaves on it.
2. Cut the stem on a slant.
3. Place a rubber or plastic hose on the cut end of the stem.
4. Fit a glass tube or straw into the end of the hose.
5. Place the glass tube or straw under water to fill it with water. Try not to get any bubbles.
6. Lay the filled tube on a table.
7. Clamp the plant to stand. (Figure 10-3.)
8. Clamp a glass or a glass chimney over the leaves.
9. Observe each day.
10. With your ruler, measure the amount of water lost from the glass tube or straw. Record your measurements each day.
11. Where has the water gone?
12. What do you notice forming on the chimney or glass over the leaves?

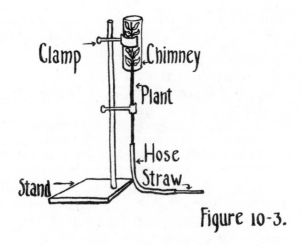

Figure 10-3.

Activity 4:   EXAMINING STOMATES

MATERIALS (per team of 2 or 3 students)

leaves from a geranium or coleus plant
dish for water
microscope

METHODS

1. Leaves from the geranium and coleus plants are good for studying the stomates. Remove a leaf from the plant.
2. Peel off some of the skin from the underside of the leaf with your fingernail.
3. Look at the spot that you peeled under the microscope. Draw and label what you see. Do NOT copy the diagram from the book. You may see something different. Draw what *YOU* see.
4. Soak one leaf in water and let another one dry out.
5. Compare and contrast the wet leaf and dry leaf under the microscope. What do you notice?
6. What causes the guard cells to open and close?

OBSERVING THAT PLANTS AND ANIMALS NEED FOOD TO LIVE

BACKGROUND

Plants and animals depend upon each other for food. Tiny plants in the sea are eaten by tiny animals and the tiny animals are eaten by small fish. The small fish are eaten by larger fish and the larger fish are caught and eaten by man. This eating of one living thing by another living thing is called a *food chain.*

For each "link" in the food chain there is energy lost. By the time man catches the big fish, 90% of the original food energy is lost. It takes energy for an animal to catch, eat, and use the food. Some of the food is wasted and is lost from the food chain. A great deal of food energy would be saved if man could gather up the tiny plants and eat them directly. (Figure 10-4.)

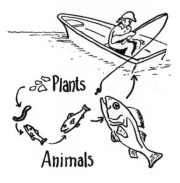

Figure 10-4. Food Chain

All food chains and food webs begin with *green* plants. As a review, ask the students if they can give a good reason for this. An example of a food web you might find on land would be: squirrels, rabbits, mice and insects eat green plants; the squirrels, rabbits and mice could all be eaten by a fox or a hawk; the insects might be eaten by a bird or a snake and the snake could be eaten by a hawk, and so on. (Figure 10-5.)

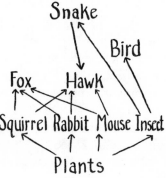

Figure 10-5. Food Web

Animals have to eat to live and often eat one another. When an animal hunts, kills, and eats another animal, this animal is called a *predator.* The animal that is eaten is the *prey.* This predator-prey relationship keeps the number of animals in both populations about the same. A *population* is a group of any one kind of plant or animal.

In the early 1900's, there was a population of about 4,000 deer living in Arizona. Many mountain lions and wolves also lived in the region. The people in the area decided to kill some of the mountain lions and wolves because they thought this action would protect the deer. Soon, the deer population grew to about 10,000 and they began to eat every shrub and seedling they could find. There wasn't enough food for all the deer and they began to die from starvation because man had changed the *balance of nature.* The deer population finally dropped to below 4,000. Could scientists have guessed that this might happen? This is a good question to stimulate class discussion.

Activity 1:   STUDYING AN ECOSYSTEM

MATERIALS (per team of 2 or 3 students)

glass jar
gauze or cloth
rubber band
aquarium tank or a box (vivarium) lined with
  aluminum foil or plastic
screen cover for aquarium or vivarium
live animals and plants

METHODS

1. Go outdoors and dig up a clump of soil from a grassy or wooded area. Keep it moist.
2. Place it in a glass jar and cover it with a piece of cloth to keep the tiny animals in the jar. (Figure 10-6.)
3. List the different plants and animals you can see and write them down in your notebook. Your ecosystem may have in it wild flowers, grasses, weeds, mosses, mushrooms, earthworms, ants, spiders, snails and mites.
4. Count the number of each kind of plant and animal you can find and record the number in your notebook too.
5. Do you see any evidence of a food chain or a food web?
6. Do you see any predator-prey relationships?
7. Count your animals and plants again after a few days. Is there any change?

Gauze

Figure 10-6. Ecosystem

RECOGNIZING HOW ANIMALS AND PLANTS INTERACT FOR BREATHING

BACKGROUND

Most living things need oxygen to breathe and respire. There are some *bacteria* however, that cannot live in oxygen. Bacteria are one-celled, plantlike *organisms,* and are so tiny that you have to look at them under a microscope that magnifies them about 1,000 times their normal size.

If plants did not produce oxygen, most organisms would die. If animals did not produce carbon dioxide, our plants might be in danger. This relationship between producing and using oxygen and carbon dioxide is called the *oxygen—carbon dioxide cycle.* (Figure 10-7.)

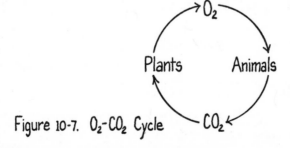

Figure 10-7. O_2-CO_2 Cycle

Plants make oxygen by using carbon dioxide, water, chlorophyll and energy from the sun. All energy originally comes from the sun. You can feel the sun's energy as heat, see it as light, or hear it as sound. Chlorophyll is the green pigment or color in plants. In some remarkable way, plants can take the carbon dioxide, water, energy, and chlorophyll and change the carbon dioxide and water into food for itself and for man and other animals. Ask the question, "Can any animal make its own food within its own body?

As the plants make food, they also make oxygen. Plants and animals use this oxygen during respiration. The oxygen helps to break down food so that each cell in the organism receives nourishment. The oxygen is taken into the cells, the food is broken down, and carbon dioxide is released. As a result of oxygen combining with the food, water and energy are formed. When oxygen combines with something else, the process is known as *oxidation*. When oxidation of food takes place, excess water and energy, in the form of heat, are given off. Ask your students to blow on their hand. What do you notice? What happens to your breath when you blow out or exhale on a cold day?

By now you probably have noticed that respiration is the opposite of photosynthesis.

$$
\underset{\text{food}}{C_6H_{12}O_{6(s)}} + \underset{\substack{\text{respiration} \longrightarrow \\ \text{gas} \\ 6O_{2(g)}}}{} \underset{\substack{\text{yields} \longrightarrow \\ \underset{\substack{\text{chlorophyll} \\ \text{and light}}}{\rightleftharpoons}}}{} 6CO_{2(g)} + 6H_2O_{(1)}
$$

sugar   +   oxygen ◄───yields   carbon dioxide   +   water
◄───photosynthesis

Green plants are able to photosynthesize and respire. Animals and plants without chlorophyll cannot carry on photosynthesis but they do respire. Scientists are working very hard to unlock the mysteries of photosynthesis. Ask your students to think for a moment and give some reasons why photosynthesis is so important. If man could make food from carbon dioxide and water, what would this mean to the people of the world? What would this mean to space travelers?

Activity 1:   BREATHING

MATERIALS (per team of 2 or 3 students)

plastic bags (11" x 12" or 27.5 cm. x 30 cm.)
thermometers (small, plastic)
blue Litmus paper

METHODS

1. Take a plastic bag about 11 inches by 12 inches (27.5 centimeters by 30 centimeters).

2. Put a small thermometer and one piece of Litmus paper in it. (Blue Litmus paper will turn red in the presence of acid.)
3. Wave the plastic bag, with the thermometer and Litmus paper in it, in the air to fill the bag.
4. Cup the bag of air over your nose and mouth and breathe normally.
5. CAUTION: When your breathing becomes difficult, STOP.
6. Remove the bag from over your mouth and nose and close the bag tightly so as not to let the gas escape from the bag.
7. How do you feel? What happened to you during this experiment? Did you notice a change in your breathing? Explain your reactions.
8. Compare your reaction with your neighbor's. Did he or she have a similar experience?

Activity 2:   RESPIRATION

MATERIALS (per team of 2 or 3 students)

plastic bag   Litmus paper
thermometer

METHODS

1. Exhale into a plastic bag as above. Examine your gas filled bag. Keep it closed tightly. What do you see in the bag? Is there any sign of moisture?
2. Open the bag. What is the reading on the thermometer? Is it the same as the temperature in the room?
3. Look at the Litmus paper. Has it changed color?
4. Explain your observations.
5. What is the difference between breathing and respiration?

Activity 3:   CHEMICAL INVESTIGATION

MATERIALS

glass   blue Litmus paper
water   straw

METHODS

1. Pour a little water into a glass.

2. Place a piece of blue Litmus paper in the water. Does the Litmus paper change color? Why?
3. Take a straw and bubble "air" into the water. Is there a change in the color of the paper now? Explain.
4. Does carbon dioxide dissolve in water?

Activity 4:   TEST FOR CARBON DIOXIDE (CO_2)

MATERIALS

glass   lime water [$Ca(OH)_2$]
water   straw

METHODS

1. Fill a glass one-half full of water.
2. Add lime water to fill the glass.
3. Take a straw and bubble the "air" from your lungs into it.
4. What happens to the lime water?
5. What is the "air" you are exhaling from your lungs?
6. Do you think your lungs are flexible like the plastic bag you used in the previous investigation?

This is the test for *carbon dioxide*. When carbon dioxide is bubbled into lime water, the lime water turns milky white. The white material is called a *precipitate* because it settles out of solution as a solid. This reaction can be written chemically as follows:

carbon	+	calcium			(marble) calcium
dioxide		hydroxide	yields	water	+ carbonate
CO_2	+	$Ca(OH)_2$	$\longrightarrow$	H_2O	+ $CaCO_3$
(g)		(l)		(l)	(s)
		lime water			white ppt.

Activity 5:   OXYGEN-CARBON DIOXIDE CYCLE

MATERIALS (per student)

determined by student

METHODS

1. Make up your own demonstration to show the oxygen-carbon dioxide cycle. What two things are essential for keeping the cycle going?

Activity 6:   PHOTOSYNTHESIS IS RESPIRATION IN REVERSE

MATERIALS (per team of 2 or 3 students)

determined by students

METHODS

1. Design an experiment that will stop a green plant from carrying on photosynthesis.
2. Since photosynthesis is a reversible reaction, do you think that a green plant could carry on respiration indefinitely if photosynthesis stops? What reasons do you have for your answer?

DETERMINING THAT ANIMALS AND PLANTS INTERACT TO REPRODUCE

BACKGROUND

All plants must reproduce to make certain that one kind of plant or animal will exist in generations to come. In order for sexual reproduction to take place, two individuals must make contact with one another in some way. When the pollen on a male plant is ripe, it has to reach the stigma of the female plant. In some cases, the pollen drops on the stigma below it. In other cases, the pollen is carried by the wind from one part of a plant to another. Animals help in the process of pollination. Bees, butterflies, moths and other insects carry pollen on their bodies from the male part of a plant to the female part. Humming birds also play a role in making sure that the pollen from one plant reaches the female part of another plant. When pollen of one plant pollinates or fertilizes another plant it is called *cross pollination.*

Activity 1:   SEEDS

MATERIALS (per student)

seeds of all types
magnifying lens or stereoscope
apple
lima beans (fresh, frozen or dried)

METHODS

A. *Seed Location*
   1. Go out into a field or wooded area.
   2. Locate as many seeds as you can find.
   3. Write down where you find each seed.
   4. How far is each seed from the parent plant?
   5. How do you think it came to be where you found it?
B. *Seed Spread*
   1. Collect as many different seeds as you can find.
   2. Identify the plant from which the seed (pit, nut, stone, bean, grain) came.
   3. Find out how the seeds from each plant are usually spread.
C. *What is an Apple?*
   1. Cut an apple in half. What do you see?
   2. Since there are seeds inside the apple, what is the fleshy part of the apple?
   3. What does the fleshy part of the apple do for the seeds?
D. *Inside a Seed.*
   1. Obtain some fresh, frozen or dried lima beans. (If you have dried beans, soak them in a little water overnight.)
   2. Peel off the outer coat of the lima bean very carefully.
   3. Examine the bean under a magnifying lens.
   4. Open the bean very carefully.
   5. Examine it again with the hand lens. (Figure 10-8.)

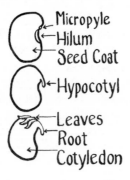

Figure 10-8. Lima Bean

   6. Draw what you see.
   7. What part do you think will become the root? The stem?
   8. The two halves of the seed are called *cotyledons.* What do you think the cotyledons do for the baby plant?

Activity 2:   MALE AND FEMALE PARTS OF FLOWERS

MATERIALS (per student)

flower in lily family (gladiola)
magnifying lens or stereoscope

METHODS

1. Obtain a flower in the lily family. (The gladiola is a good example.)
2. Carefully peel off the petals and expose the reproductive organs. (Figure 10-9.)

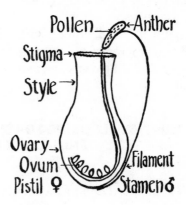

Figure 10-9. Flower

The thin filaments have an *anther* on the top which produces the powdery pollen. The filament and anther make up the male reproductive part of the plant called the *stamen*. The vaselike structure in the center is the female part called the *pistil*. The base is the *ovary* where the seeds are formed. The thin neck is the *style* and at the top of the style is the *stigma*. The pollen falls on the sticky stigma and travels down the style to the ovary. The pollen fertilizes the eggs (ova or seeds) in the ovary and the seed grows.

3. Examine the flower parts with a hand lens or under a stereoscope.
4. Draw and label the flower.
5. Why do plants need flowers?
6. What does the ovary do?

All animals must reproduce to make certain that a particular type of animal will exist in generations to come. Many animals use some kind of plant material in building nests or homes where eggs are laid or young animals are raised. In some cases, fertilization itself takes place in the nests.

Female birds lay their eggs in nests made of bits of plant material. Rabbits make nests of plant material, paper, and string. These materials make a soft, warm bed for the baby animals when they are born.

The male stickleback fish builds a nest of plant material on a sandy bottom. He then leads a female fish to the nest. When she enters the nest, the male fish pokes her tail several times to urge her to lay her eggs. After the female fish lays the eggs, she swims away. The male then enters the nest and releases sperm, the male sex cells, that fertilize the eggs.

Trees, bushes and other plants also provide support for animal nests. Plants interact with animals for reproduction by providing the material for building nests and support for holding the nests once they are built.

Activity 3:   LOOKING FOR EVIDENCE OF PLANT AND ANIMAL INTERACTION

MATERIALS (per team of 2 or 3 students)

notebook
resource materials

METHODS

1. Take a field trip to locate as many different kinds of nests that are built with plant materials.
2. Write down where you find each nest, its size, and describe what it looks like.
3. Try to determine which animal built the nest.
4. Does the animal select plant material from a particular tree or bush for his nest?

Activity 4:   INVESTIGATING WAYS ANIMALS INTERACT TO REPRODUCE

MATERIALS

library resources

METHODS

1. Go to the library. Use all the library materials available to find out about nesting, courtship, and the mating habits of some of the wild animals in your region of the country.

KEY POINTS

Key Points and Activities

(1) Build a diorama or a mural of a particular area in your school yard or a nearby pond. Include the plants and animals normally found in the school yard or pond. Do some reading in the libary on the plants and animals of the area. Be sure to place them on your diorama or mural where they are most likely to be found in nature. When you have finished, remove one of the plants or animals from your picture and guess what would happen to the food chain with one of the links missing. Add a new plant or animal to the system. In each example, explain what you think will happen orally or in writing.

(2) Visit a river. List and describe the major plants and animals that live there. What relationship does one living thing have to another?

(3) Label three large test tubes "A," "B" and "C." Place a piece of crumbled paper in the bottom of each. Add water enough to soak the paper in each tube.
Place a small plant in tube "A." Plug the tube with a rubber stopper. (Figure 10-10.)

Figure 10-10.

A — Plant, Wet paper

B — Sugar strip, Fly, Wet paper

C — Sugar strip, Plant and fly, Wet paper

Soak a small strip of paper toweling in sugar syrup and place it on the side of tube "B." Put a small animal such as a fly, in the tube and stopper it. The sugar is food for the animal.

Into the tube labeled "C," place a plant as in "A" and a sugar soaked strip and an animal as in "B." Stopper.

Observe what happens in each test tube after 30 minutes. Observe again the next day. Record all your observations. What does this experiment show? Explain and use diagrams to show how the plant and animal interact in this experiment. What happens when an animal must live without plants? What happens when a plant must live without animals?

(4) Suppose all the animals on earth were to suddenly die. There would be no more carbon dioxide produced by animals. What would happen to the green plants that need carbon dioxide for photosynthesis? Are there other sources of carbon dioxide?

(5) If photosynthesis is the opposite of respiration, or respiration in reverse, how is it that plants still need the carbon dioxide produced by animals?

(6) Make a large chart of plants and animals that depend on each other to help insure that there will be a new generation in the future. Draw arrows between plants and animals that interact with one another. Remove one plant or animal from your chart and guess what would happen.

(7) Make a study of how man has changed the way plants and animals interact and reproduce. For example, you may wish to know more about how and why scientists experiment with pollination and the cross pollination of plants. Why would they want to cross one kind of wheat plant, corn or peach tree with another variety of wheat, corn or peach? You may prefer to find out how and why scientists experiment with breeding animals or why they study populations and overpopulation.

GLOSSARY

acid — a substance that burns the skin, is sour to the taste, and turns blue Litmus paper red.

anther — the male part of a flower that produces pollen.

balance of nature — balance means even or the same, and therefore, a balance in nature refers to the number of plants, animals and resources staying about the same. Often, when man tries to control the environment or nature, he upsets the balance of plants, animals and the non-living environment.

breathing — the mechanical way living things take in oxygen and give off carbon dioxide. For example, humans breathe with lungs, fish breathe with gills.

chlorophyll — the green coloring of plants—green pigment.

cotyledons — the two halves of a seed that provide the baby plant with food until it can carry on photosynthesis and make its own food.

cross pollination — the process by which one plant fertilizes another plant. The pollen of one plant is used to pollinate another plant.

element — one kind of atom. For example, carbon is made up of only carbon atoms.

food chain — a step-by-step transfer of food energy, such as tiny animals eating tiny plants, and larger animals eating smaller animals.

food web — a branched food chain with many different animals eating plants and smaller animals.

formula — the chemical name for a substance.

guard cells — two cells around the stomates of leaves that open and close the pores.

interact — to have an effect on, or influence each other.

nourishment — foodlike material that can be used for growth by something that is living.

nutrient — food material.

organism — any living individual plant or animal.

ova — eggs or seeds.

ovary — the female part of a flower that holds the eggs (ova or seeds).

oxidation — the combining of oxygen with something else—slow or rapid burning or combustion.

oxygen-carbon dioxide cycle — the continuous formation of oxygen and carbon dioxide by plants and animals.

photosynthesis — the making of food by green plants from carbon dioxide and water with energy from light.

pistil — the female part of the flower which contains the stigma, style and ovary.

pollination — the depositing of pollen on the sticky top section of the female part of a flower.

population — a group of any one kind of plant or animal.

predator — an animal that hunts and kills another animal for food.

prey — an animal that is killed and eaten for food.

root hair — a root cell with a piece that is stretched out to take in water.

sperm — the sex cells of the male animal.

stamen — the male part of a flower that holds the anther.

stigma — the sticky top section of the female part of a flower.

stomate — a pore or opening on leaves of green plants.

style — the female part of the flower between the stigma and ovary.

tadpole — a young frog that still lives in the water and breathes with gills.

transpiration — the loss of water by a plant through the pores.

BIBLIOGRAPHY

Mark, Steven J. *Science Through Experiments*. Illinois: Benefic Press, 1971.

Odum, Eugene P. *Ecology*. New York: Holt, Rinehart and Winston, 1963.

Parker, B. M. and Ralph Buchsbaum. *Balance in Nature*. New York: Harper and Row, 1965.

Parker, Bertha Morris. *Plant and Animal Partnerships*. New York: Row, Peterson & Co., 1961.

Rasmussen, F. A., P. Holobinko, and V. M. Showalter. *Man and His Environment*. Boston: Houghton-Mifflin Co., 1971.
Smith, Robert L. *Ecology and Field Biology*. New York: Harper and Row, 1966.
Thurber, Walter A. and Robert E. Kilburn. *Exploring Life Science*. Boston: Allyn and Bacon, Inc. 1967.

11

Observing Populations, Communities and Ecosystems

INVESTIGATING THE BIOTIC COMMUNITY IN THE SAME HABITAT

BACKGROUND

By now, your students should realize that *ecology* is the study of living things, their relationship to each other and to their environment. Life exists in the lowest atmosphere, in a few feet below the earth surface and in bodies of water. This area in which life exists is called the *biosphere*. *Ecosystems* exist within this area wherever an environment is stable, where living and nonliving things interact, and also, where materials are recycled, that is, used over and over again. The life in an ecosystem is referred to as the *biotic community,* and the nonliving components or the physical part as the *abiotic environment*. Three kinds of relationships exist in an ecosystem: (1) the interaction of living things with one another; (2) the interaction of living things with the physical environment; and (3) the interaction of abiotic factors with one another. A group of individuals of any one kind living within an ecosystem is called a *population*. The place where an organism or a population lives is his *habitat*.

Investigating the biotic community in the same habitat, then, refers to the living things which live in a particular place. Hence, in studying a particular community, the limits of the ecosystem must be defined. Have your students select different types of ecosystems—an open field or clearing, a wooded area, a ravine, a swamp, and so on, and then have them follow the procedure below.

Activity 1: DETERMINING THE BIOTIC COMMUNITY IN THE SAME HABITAT

MATERIALS (per team of 2 or 3 students)

meter stick   4 stakes
string   pencil and paper

METHODS

1. Stake out 1 meter (or 1 yard) square as your ecosystem.
2. Describe your ecosystem. Is it made up mostly of plants or animals? What is the physical environment like? Is it rocky, hilly, sandy, wet, dry, or what?
3. Count the number of different kinds of plants that occupy the same habitat. Identify as many as you can, at least in large catagories, such as, ferns, mosses, algae, fungi, lichens, flowering and nonflowering plants, etc.

DETERMINING THE DOMINANT POPULATION WITHIN A COMMUNITY

BACKGROUND

The dominant population within a community is determined by the number of organisms of any one kind present. The organisms most abundant comprise the population that is *dominant* in a community. There are several ways to make quantitative studies of populations of plants and animals. One way is to remove them all and count them. Another way to count the number of animals is to use the *sweep method* whereby you sweep an area with a net several times. These procedures are described below.

Activity 1: REMOVING AND COUNTING PLANTS IN A QUADRAT

MATERIALS (per class)

meter stick   4 stakes
string   pencil and paper

METHODS

1. Stake out 1 meter square (or 1 yard square) as you did in the previous activity or use one of the most interesting quadrats you staked out before. (A quadrat is a sample plot that is a square.)
2. Remove all the plants from the quadrat, place them in collecting pans, and carry them into the laboratory.
3. Form teams and let one team sort out the plants, another team count them, and a third, identify them.
4. Record:

a. Description of Quadrat.
b. Location of Quadrat.
c. Total number of plants per meter square in Quadrat A:

$$\text{Density} = \frac{\text{Total \# of plants}}{\text{Total sample area in square meters}}$$

d. Number of different kinds of plants in Quadrat A:

$$\text{Density} = \frac{\text{Total \# of each species}}{\text{Total sample area in square meters}}$$

e. Dominant population of plants in Quadrat A.
f. List names of plants identified.

Activity 2: REMOVING AND COUNTING ANIMALS WITHIN A LIMITED AREA

MATERIALS (per class)

large bag or large shallow box
chloroform or ether
cotton
plastic containers with covers

METHODS

1. Saturate several wads of cotton with ether or chloroform and place in the bag or box. Close the container and let the anesthesia permeate the container for about 1 minute.
2. Open the container and quickly turn it over onto the ground and allow to stay for one or two minutes. The ether or chloroform will anesthetize the tiny animals trapped beneath the container.

3. Carefully pick up the animals and place in the plastic container and cover.
4. Repeat the procedure several times until you think you have captured all the animals in that small area.
5. Measure the area covered by the bag or box so you can determine the number of animals found within a defined space.
6. Carry the specimens back to the laboratory.
7. As before, form teams and let one team sort the animals, another count them and the third, identify them. (If the animals begin to revive before you sort them, hold a piece of cotton saturated with the anesthetic in the container over the animals. Do not touch them. Ether and chloroform will "burn" them on contact.)
8. Record:
   a. Description of Area.
   b. Location of Area.
   c. Size of Area.
   d. Total number of animals in area:

$$\text{Density} = \frac{\text{Total \# of animals}}{\text{Total sample area}}$$

   e. Number of different kinds of animals in area.
   f. Dominant population of animals in area.
   g. List names of animals identified.

Activity 3:   USING THE SWEEP METHOD FOR COLLECTING ANIMALS

MATERIALS (per team of 2 or 3 students)

insect net   4 stakes
killing jar   string
ether or chloroform

METHODS

1. Mark off 100 meters square (or yards square).
2. In an orderly fashion, walk the area and sweep the ground vegetation with a back and forth stroke.
2. Count the number of strokes and record them.
4. Place the captured animals in a covered container or a killing jar and after anesthetizing them, count them. Label them the "First Removal Sample."

5. Repeat the sweep using the same number of strokes and count again. Label. Repeat several times.
6. Plot on a graph the number of animals collected in each sample. With each collection, the number of animals should lessen. You should notice a ratio between trials and thus, you can estimate the total number of animals in the ecosystem.

OBSERVING FOOD RELATIONSHIPS—IDENTIFYING THE FOOD CHAIN AND FOOD WEB

BACKGROUND

If your students were acutely alert to the interaction of the living things in the ecosystems they studied in the previous activities in this chapter, they may have seen plants being eaten by animals, and small animals being eaten by larger animals. If so, they were observing a step in a *food chain* process. Unless one is observing a closed environment, it is difficult to observe a total chain of one living thing eating another and then, being eaten by still another. There are many types of food chains but they all have the same pattern, that is, green plants are eaten by herbivores, herbivores are eaten by carnivores and carnivores are eaten by larger carnivores until the largest carnivore is reached in a particular chain. Some chains are short and some are long. In a grassland, the chain could be grass——→cattle——→man. In Africa, it could be grass——→zebra——→lion. In a meadow, the chain might be a little longer, grass——→cricket——→frog——→snake——→ hawk. In a pond, it might be algae——→protozoan——→insect——→ bass——→pickerel. In the sea it might be phytoplankton——→zoo-plankton——→small fish——→larger fish and possibly man as the top *predator*.

Food webs are a little more complicated because in such relationships, the predators eat several kinds of food and every kind of food is eaten by many different predators. If you identify all the food chains in a given community and diagram them together, you will have a food web.

Activity 1:   IDENTIFYING FOOD CHAINS AND CONSTRUCTING FOOD WEBS

MATERIALS (per team of 2 or 3 students)

paper and pencil

METHODS

1. Select a biotic community you can observe over a period of time, such as an open field, bog, marsh, pond, etc.
2. Identify a green plant and observe animals feeding on it.
3. Using the observed animal and plant as the first link in the food chain, construct the rest of the chain.
4. Select another plant and proceed as above.
5. When you have constructed several food chains, diagram them all on a large piece of paper and show how they all comprise a partial food web for that community.
6. What would happen if one link in a particular chain became extinct?

If you wish to supplement Activity 1 and give your students daily experience in observing a food chain in the classroom, have the students set up a terrarium. They will have to learn what to put into it and how to care for it. They will also realize the importance of environmental factors such as temperature, moisture, and acidity as well as the food habits of the living things. Perhaps one of the easiest terrariums to maintain is a semi-aquatic one in which a variety of plants can be planted and several animals can be introduced.

Select a large terrarium case. A regular terrarium or 10 gallon (30.785 liters) aquarium can be used. Place gravel in the bottom of the terrarium and cover it with sand. Build up one end with acid soil leaving the lower end to be filled with water. Add enough soil so there is a gradual incline to the water, and so that the water can be 15 to 20 cm. high. Plant some Bladderwort, Elodea and Ludwigia in the water; some Sphagnum moss, ferns, and lichens on the shore line; and some Venus' flytrap plants, Pitcher plants, and other bog plants in the upper portion of the land area. Place Dragonfly and Damselfly larvae, tadpoles, minnows, sunfish and crayfish in the water. Add newts, turtles, small water snakes, tree frogs, bullfrogs, and leopard frogs, young and old, to the land area. Also add living insects, fruit flies, blow flies, June bugs, house flies, grasshoppers, caterpillars, mealworms, and earthworms. These will offer plenty of food for the larger animals. Before adding any artificial food, have the students observe the terrarium for several days to identify food chains. They should see bullfrogs eating the minnows, crayfish, and young leopard frogs, as well as insects and worms. The leopard frog will consume the worms and the insects and so will the tree frogs. The tadpoles will eat the algae in the water. The turtle will seek out the fish, tadpoles, aquatic insects, mealworms and earthworms.

Place the terrarium in a cool place and observe daily.

**Activity 2:   USING A TERRARIUM TO STUDY FOOD CHAINS
AND FOOD WEBS**

MATERIALS

4 liter terrarium or aquarium with wire cover
thermometer
gravel
sand
acid soil
plants: Bladderwort, Elodea, Ludwigia, Sphagnum moss, ferns,
          lichens, Venus' flytrap, Pitcher plants
animals: Dragonfly larvae, Damselfly larvae, tadpoles, minnows,
          sunfish, crayfish, newts, turtles, water snake, tree frogs,
          bullfrog, leopard frogs, fruit flies, blow flies, June bugs,
          flies, grasshoppers, caterpillars, mealworms, earthworms

METHODS

1. Look up information about the different types of terraria you
   can have in a classroom—desert, woodland, bog, semi-aquatic,
   etc.—and decide on the one you want to construct to study food
   chains and food webs. The materials listed above are for a semi-
   aquatic terrarium.
2. Identify which food chains you might observe and select the
   appropriate plants and animals for your tank.
3. Construct your terrarium based on what you have read or found
   out.
4. Observe your terrarium daily and record your observations
   making note of observed links in a particular food chain.
5. After a few weeks or when your food chains are completed,
   diagram them on a large piece of paper.
   Is there any link missing?
   Can you identify the food web in your terrarium?
6. Do all your food chains begin with a green plant? Is the Venus'
   flytrap a producer or consumer?
7. Remove a link in one of the food chains and observe what
   happens for three days. Replace the missing link and observe for
   another three days. What do you think is most significant about
   this experiment?

DETERMINING THE STABILITY OF A COMMUNITY (NUMBER)

BACKGROUND

There are three basic factors that maintain stability within a community. They are food supply, birth and death, and protection. If a food supply is abundant, an individual species of animals will move in. This ultimately depends on the plant growth, for the green plant is at the start of any food chain. As herbivores consume the green plants they attract carnivores. If more carnivores moved in than there were herbivores, some carnivores would starve, upsetting the stability of the community. This often happens as a normal course of events but over a period of time and many fluctuations, the balance in nature is maintained unless there is some outside interference.

One of our big concerns today is a situation that potentially threatens a normal food cycle, and that is the 800 mile pipeline from the oil fields of the North Slope region of Alaska across the country to Valdez in the southern section. It is feared that even with every precaution taken, there will be spillage and oil will seep over the land and into the ocean. This will result in contamination of fish and game and more importantly, will also contaminate and kill the plankton, the basic food of the fish and a basic supply of oxygen. If the fish die so will the seals and walruses that feed upon them. If the seals and walruses die, the Eskimos will have lost their own major sources of food.

Animals are born, plants sprout—and both grow, mature, reproduce in most cases, and eventually die. This is the normal life and death cycle which usually is balanced. As one individual dies another is born. Only man, through his manipulation of the environment, has disrupted the normal balance of plants and animals. For example, man raises crops purposely for food, and grazes cattle for the same reason. Man also has domesticated animals as pets and caused an overpopulation of cats and dogs. One occasionally hears of a pack of stray dogs which have herded together to forage for themselves across the land. And one need only to visit the Colosseum in Rome to see abandoned "shrunken lions" basking in the sun! Man himself has reproduced at such a staggering rate that many population experts fear that we have seriously disturbed man's balance with nature.

All living things are interdependent in some way and each species has some protective device for self-survival and for survival of the species. For example, zebras, giraffes and antelopes can often be seen together because they help protect each other from lions and other predators. Giraffes have height and keen eyesight. Antelopes have excellent hearing and the zebra has a sharp sense of smell. Together, they form a team dependent upon each other for survival. Man, too, is dependent upon others for survival, and his own protective device—his ability to think and reason—is crying out that man is doomed unless he restores the imbalances he has caused or allowed to happen.

In order to help your students better understand how nature maintains a dynamic stability within and among living systems, let them study the relationships within a designated *biome*. Perhaps you can enlist the assistance of a resource person from a nearby nature center or college to help with Activity 1. As a culminating activity, have the students discuss the consequences of the Alaskan pipeline. You might even want them to do this as a case study and have them role play.

Activity 1: STUDYING THE IMMIGRATION AND EMIGRATION OF ANIMALS IN AN ECOSYSTEM

MATERIALS (per class)

rope
dye, tags or animal bands

METHODS (obtain assistance from someone who has done this before

1. Rope off a rather large measured area.
2. By using nets and harmless animal traps, capture the animals in the area, tag them with dye or tags, or band them so you will recognize them again. Then set them free. Record the number of animals present.
3. After a few days, capture the animals again and determine the ratio of marked animals to the unmarked ones. This will give you an indication of the migration of animals in and out of an area.
4. Did the total number of animals remain about the same? Did you find entirely different types of animals or were they, on the whole, the same?

Activity 2: CONSEQUENCES OF THE ALASKAN OIL PIPELINE

MATERIALS

References and resource material on the Alaskan Pipeline from the oil fields on the North Slope of Alaska.

METHODS

1. Form two teams. One team will search for reasons supporting the pipeline and the other will search for reasons against the pipeline.
2. After an extensive review of the literature on the Alaskan pipeline, select a committee of four, two from each team, to conduct a hearing where each side is to present its case.
3. At the close of discussion, the committee of four will make recommendations based on the testimony given. If any appropriate action can be taken, it should be done as a unified proposal from the whole class.

INVESTIGATING SUCCESSION WITHIN THE COMMUNITY

BACKGROUND

Succession has been discussed in Chapter 7; however, it bears repeating here. Succession takes place over a period of time and is a gradual replacement of one community with another until a stable equilibrium is reached. Each living population occupying an ecosystem changes the *micro-climate,* that is, the local conditions (light, temperature, acidity, alkalinity). In turn the substrate or the abiotic environment changes the conditions for life and hence, the plants and animals living in the area. Sometimes these changes take place over ten to twenty years, other times over one hundred years or more. It isn't necessary for your students to wait several years to observe succession. They can do so in the plot of land they defoliated in *Activity 1: Removing and Counting Plants in a Quadrat.* Have them observe the plot daily and record the changes that take place. Be sure it is left undisturbed so that succession can take place naturally.

Succession can also be studied in the laboratory by conducting a simple experiment. Have the students perform the activities below to observe succession within a confined community.

Activity 1:   OBSERVING SUCCESSION IN A POND WATER COMMUNITY

MATERIALS (per team of 2 or 3 students)

3 flasks   microscope
   hydrion or litmus paper   light meter

glass slides   medicine droppers
thermometer   hay infusion or grass

METHODS

1. Fill 3 flasks 1/2 full with pond water and label them "A," "B" and "C."
2. Add a little hay infusion or grass to each flask.
3. Place one flask (C) in the refrigerator or in a cool place, and leave the other two (A & B) together at room temperature.
4. Take the temperature of the cultures and record.

    A_____.
    B_____.
    C_____.

5. Record the pH of each.

    A_____.
    B_____.
    C_____.

6. Place the light meter in front of each culture and record.

    A_____.
    B_____.
    C_____.

7. Place 5 drops of pond water on a slide and examine under a microscope. Record as follows:

	A	B	C
a. Number of organisms in 5 drops:	—	—	—
b. Number of different organisms:	—	—	—

    c. Draw and label as many different organisms as you can.

8. Repeat the above every three days and record your observations. Does the temperature change? If so, what might be the cause? Does the pH change? If so, due to what factors? Does the culture become more or less dense as measured by the light meter? Does the number of organisms change? Does the number of different organisms change? Have you been able to observe succession in process? How does the cold culture (C) compare and contrast with the one kept at room temperature?
9. Plot the results of your observations (temperature, pH, density, number of organisms, number of different organisms) on graph paper.

10. Do the physical factors or abiotic elements affect the stability within a community? Do the living things or biotic elements affect the stability within a community? How are they interrelated as seen on your graph?

PREDICTING WHAT WILL HAPPEN TO THE FLOW OF MATERIALS AND ENERGY WHEN THE SYSTEM IS THREATENED

BACKGROUND

The number of organisms and their metabolic activity depend upon the rate at which energy flows through the *trophic* or feeding levels and upon the rate at which materials circulate through a system. This applies equally to all organisms and all environments, and thus, two general laws or principles can be applied to the study of ecology. One law states that the flow of energy through a biological system is one way and is reduced with each succeeding trophic level. The second law refers to the circulation of raw materials. Raw materials are not lost to the system but can be used again. Energy is lost from the system but matter is recycled.

This energy and food intake and transfer occurs in food chains and food webs within ecological communities. Raw materials are used by green plants, are transferred to a higher feeding or trophic level when eaten by herbivores, and then by carnivores, and eventually, are decomposed and returned to the soil as water, carbon dioxide, elemental carbon, nitrogen, phosphorous, sulfur, calcium, and so on.

Let's trace the movement of raw materials through the trophic levels along food chains of predator-prey relationships using a forest ecosystem as an example.

As you know, all food chains and food webs begin with green plants. Green plants capture the sun's energy and, using chlorophyll as a catalyst, convert carbon dioxide and water to food and oxygen. The rate of photosynthesis is important in determining how much life can be supported. Remember, much of the material produced by plants is also used by them and only about 10% can be transferred when eaten by herbivores. The sun's energy and the rate of photosynthesis then, are limiting factors in predicting the amount of food and energy that is contained in an ecosystem. Other limiting factors include the materials available such as, water, carbon dioxide, oxygen, nitrogen, sulfur, etc.

The first trophic level is made up of the primary consumers or herbivores. In the forest ecosystem, these herbivores are birds which eat seeds, buds and foliage; insects which eat all parts of the plants; deer and rabbits which eat twigs and leaves, and gophers which eat the roots of plants.

In the second trophic level, the secondary consumers are carnivores which eat the animals in the first trophic level. The carnivores in the forest include hawks, owls, foxes, shrews, skunks, snakes, scavengers, birds, and insect eating insects.

A hawk is also a tertiary consumer because he is a carnivore which consumes snakes and weasels. In some ecosystems, fourth level consumers also exist. For example, scavengers will eat dead hawks.

In addition to *herbivores* (plant eaters), and *carnivores* (animal eaters), there are *omnivores* and *cannibals.* Omnivores will eat plants and animals and cannibals eat one another. Mice will do the latter just to supplement their diet. The Eastern red fox is an omnivore because he eats mice, rabbits, birds, lizards, other small animals, and also, fruits and seeds. Bears eat small mammals, snakes, fish, grasses, berries, fruits, leaves, bark and picnic lunches! Of course man too, is an omnivore because he eats meat, vegetables, fruits and nuts.

In the final trophic level, we find the decomposers. Decomposers, primarily bacteria and fungi (yeasts and molds), break up dead animals, plants, and waste material into simpler form and these compounds and elements are then used again by plants and are also recycled through the biological system.

In the predator - prey relationship, any organism is a potential prey of organisms in the trophic level above it. Organisms occupying the same trophic level are competitors for the same food supply. Have your students keep these factors in mind when they study and try to measure the relationships in any ecosystem whether it be a forest, grass prairie, desert, pond, ocean, or coral atoll.

To illustrate food chains and a food web, have your students present this visually. You'll need a ball of twine and some index cards. Write the names of the predators and preys on individual cards and follow the activity below. After this exercise, the students should be able to predict what will happen when a link in the food chain or food web is removed.

Make up cards for two simple food chains first then for a food web. For example, one chain could be clover⎯⎯▸cow⎯⎯▸man. Write each name on a separate card. Another chain could be grass⎯⎯▸grasshopper⎯⎯▸mice⎯⎯▸hawk. Write these on cards too. For the food web, you can include: grass, crops, and trees in the primary trophic level; grasshoppers, rabbits, woodchucks, and deer in the secondary trophic level; mice, men, and mountain lions in the tertiary trophic level; snakes and owls in the quarternary trophic level; and scavengers and decomposers in the final trophic level.

Activity 1:　PREDICTING WHAT WILL HAPPEN WHEN A SYSTEM IS THREATENED

MATERIALS (per class)

ball of twine

index cards with names of individual members of a food chain or food web.

METHODS

1. Each person should take a card with the name of a plant or animal on it for a particular food chain.
2. Take one end of a piece of twine and connect the predator - preys beginning with the primary producer and extending it to the last consumer.
3. Remove one member in the chain.
4. Predict what will happen to the food materials and transfer of matter and energy in the system.
5. What will happen to the rest of the organisms in the food chain?
6. What could this do to the balance in nature?
7. Repeat the above using another food chain or a food web.
8. What would happen in the forest ecosystem described previously if:

   a. An organism were removed?
   b. A raw material, such as water, carbon-dioxide, nitrogen, phosphorous, sulfur or calcium was not available?
   c. The amount of sunlight was reduced?

Now, let's look into the flow of energy through the biological system. The sun is our ultimate and continuous source of energy, and fortunately for us, it is a continuous source because the energy flow through a biological system is one-directional. Energy comes directly from the ffun and is dissipated into space as a result of biological respiration and heat loss. Energy is not recirculated. The flow of energy in a community is governed by two important laws of thermodynamics. The first is that the amount of energy in the universe is constant—energy can be transformed and transferred but is neither gained nor lost. The second law states that when energy is transformed or transferred, part of the energy assumes a form that cannot be passed on any further and is dissipated into the atmosphere as heat.

If we trace this process, we find that approximately 57% of the sun's energy is scattered in space and also absorbed by the atmosphere. About 36% is expended to heat the land and to heat and evaporate water. Energy from the decaying process heats the ground so not too much of the sun's energy is absorbed by the land. Only 8% of solar radiation actually strikes the plant life and 10 - 15% of this 8% is reflected, 5% is transmitted, and 80 - 85% is absorbed. Of the 80 - 85% absorbed, only 0.5 - 3.5% is used in the photosynthetic process, and the greater part of it is lost as heat and in the evaporation of water. This obviously is not very efficient use of the sun's vast energy supply.

The energy flow through an ecosystem follows a general rule, that is, the energy available decreases by a factor of 100 from the producers to the primary consumer and then by a factor of 10 for each additional transfer to succeeding trophic levels. For example, it would take 10,000 pounds or 4,500 kilograms of green plants to feed 100 pounds or 45 kilograms of insects; 100 pounds of insects to feed 10 pounds or 4.5 kilograms of frogs; and 10 pounds of frogs to feed 1 pound or .45 kilograms of water snakes. This is not total weight either, but refers only to the stored proteins, carbohydrates and fats. Obviously, 100% of energy is not passed on from level to level. In fact, the efficiency of transfer is 10%. Some energy is used by the organisms themselves for life processes—respiration, locomotion and so forth. The number of organisms (also referred to as the *standing crop*) therefore, also decreases with each additional feeding level or link in a food chain. There are many more producers than tertiary consumers, for instance. Make it clear to your students that feeding levels, or trophic classification, is one of function, not of species. As seen in the above forest ecosystem, a given species may occupy one or more trophic levels. Also, the shorter the food chain, the greater the available food energy. For practical purposes, the food chain is limited to only three or four links. Much beyond this, there is hardly any energy left to transfer. If 1500 Calories of the sun's energy are absorbed by green plants per square meter per day, the plants net only 15 Calories. Of this energy, the primary consumers receive only 1.5 Calories and transfer but 0.15 Calories. Remember too, there is much waste in addition to plants and animals using some of the energy to carry on their own life processes. Some energy is dissipated as heat and some energy is lost in the parts of the plants and animals that are left behind by consumers.

As the energy decreases with each successive trophic level, so does the standing crop or the *biomass*. The standing crop biomass is usually expressed in terms of grams of organic matter, grams of carbon, or Calories per unit area (square meter, hectare). Biomass determination follows the Inverse Size-Metabolic Rate "law," which states that, in general, the smaller the organism, the greater the metabolic rate per gram of weight. Biomass, therefore, is influenced by the size of the organism in a particular trophic level. It is possible to obtain as much food from mass cultures of algae as from a crop of grain.

If we could increase the amount of energy absorbed by green plants and increase the rate of photosynthesis, overall productivity could be increased. Such experiments have been conducted with algae. Large vats of algae have been exposed to light for extended periods of time in hope that they would produce more food faster. Results, however, were disappointing. Photosynthesis was increased just so much and then the algal production leveled off. Much more research is needed in this area to increase food productivity.

The following activities can be performed to help the students better understand the concept of biomass and how total amounts can be determined and potential productivity estimated. To determine Total Biomass, both activities should be carried out on the same plot of land and simultaneously.

Activity 2:   DETERMINING THE BIOMASS OF PLANTS

MATERIALS (per class)

    measuring tape
4 stakes
    ball of twine

METHODS

1. Measure off 1 meter square of land.
2. Remove all the plants from the quadrat and carry them back to the laboratory.
3. Spread the plants out to dry directly in the sun, in a warm place, or in a drying oven.
4. When the plants are dry, remove the soil from the roots and weigh the plants.
5. The weight of organic matter represents the biomass or standing crop of plants per square meter of land.
               Biomass=____grams

Before you perform Activity 3, discuss the consequences of this experiment with your students. Is the activity essential to their understanding of biomass and total biomass? If not, should the animals be sacrificed just because the activity is included in the book? What purpose will it serve and is it justified? In some cases the answer will be "yes," and in others, "no."

Activity 3:   DETERMINING THE BIOMASS OF ANIMALS

MATERIALS (per class)

measuring tape
4 stakes
ball of twine
cotton

box, 1/2 meter on each side
of opening
chloroform or ether
containers with covers

METHODS

1. Measure the opening of the box.
2. Saturate some cotton with chloroform or ether and let permeate throughout the box.
3. Tip the box upside down over the ground to anesthetize the animals underneath.
4. Remove the box and the animals. Place the animals in containers, cover them, and carry them back to the laboratory.
5. Saturate cotton with anesthesia and hold in the containers until you are certain the animals have expired.
6. Place the dead animals directly in the sun, or in a warm place to dry out. If a drying oven or regular stove oven is available, place them in an aluminum plate and dry them in the oven.
7. When the animals are dried out, let them coof off, then weigh the total mass.
8. The weight of organic matter represents the biomass or standing crop of animals per area of land.
   If the box did have an opening with 1/2 meter on the open side, multiply the biomass by 2 in order to get the biomass weight per square meter of land.

   Biomass=____grams

If you want your students to determine the total biomass for a given plot of land, be sure they take the plants and animals from the same quadrat. The biomass determined for plants and the biomass for animals should then be added together.

$$\text{Biomass}_P + \text{Biomass}_A = \text{Total Biomass per area of land}$$

KEY POINTS

Key Points and Activities

Many of these terms will be a review. Make a point to have students use them in their daily discussions.

ecology	food web
biosphere	terrarium
ecosystem	food supply
biotic community	birth and death
abiotic environment	protection
population	succession
community	microclimate
habitat	trophic or feeding levels
"sweep" method	omnivore
quadrat	cannibal
herbivore	decomposer
carnivore	standing crop or biomass
food chain	

As an extended activity, your students may enjoy illustrating the food web of the forest ecosystem as described in this chapter. They can make mobiles, make a diorama and attach strings to each organism showing the predator-prey relationships and trophic levels, or even draw a complex chart.

As another activity to see if your students truly understand the flow of energy and materials through biological systems, ask them to draw a diagram or flow chart combining all they learned from that section in the chapter. An illustration of this is included for your perusal. (Figure 11-1.)

GLOSSARY

biomass — the living weight per unit area, or the mass of all the living material within a measured amount of space.

biome — a large geographic area of one climate and which may have a number of different communities, and which frequently can be identified by its climax vegetation i.e., desert biome, tundra biome, grasslands biome.

carnivore — an animal eater.

herbivore — a plant eater.

omnivore — eats both plants and animals.

quadrat — a sample plot that is a square. The denser the area the larger the quadrat should be.

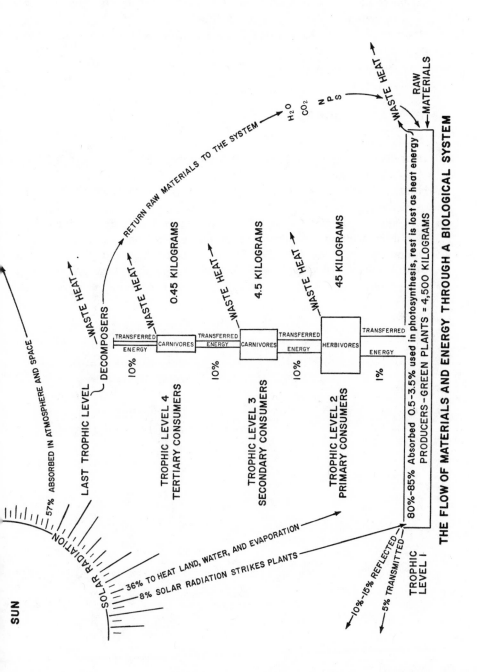

Figure 11-1.

shrunken lions — term used by tour guides to describe the stray cats that now inhabit the Colosseum in Rome.

standing crop — the amount of living material in the different trophic levels.

trophic levels — feeding levels in a producer-consumer or herbivore-carnivore food chain.

BIBLIOGRAPHY

Buchsbaum, Ralph and Mildred. *Basic Ecology.* Pittsburgh, Pennsylvania: The Boswood Press, 1957.

Hurdle, William R. *Ecology Experienced.* Saginaw, Michigan: Trippensee Publishing, 1973.

McCombs, Lawrence G., and Nicholas Rosa. *What's Ecology?* Reading, Massachusetts: Addison-Wesley Publishing Company, 1973.

Odum, Eugene P. *Ecology.* New York: Holt, Rinehart and Winston, 1963.

Smith, Robert L. *Ecology and Field Biology.* New York: Harper and Row, 1966.

12

Things That Pollute Our Land

BACKGROUND

Solid waste disposal has been a problem since ancient times, only years ago, there was more space to throw things away. Today the problem is made worse by increased populations, by crowding in the cities, and by the fact that, as former Governor William T. Cahill of New Jersey has said, there just is no "away" any more. Wherever there are people, there is going to be litter and garbage. When people had room to spread out, and when the majority of people were farmers, they returned to the land what they took from it. Composting was a part of their daily routine. Animal and household wastes were buried in the ground where they would decay, allowing the raw materials to return to the soil to be recirculated through the biological system. It was good for the crops, and it was a means of getting rid of unwanted rubbish.

Our current problem is compounded because we have so many more things to discard and our whole way of life has changed. At one time, it was a sign of thrift if one took care of material things and repaired them when needed. Now-a-days, we manufacture products for obsolescence. When they break down, we throw them out. Gone are the days when your refrigerator would last thirty years as have some of the old monitor top models. Gone are the days when you could expect a bicycle to last a child through all of his growing years.

213

It apparently is cheaper to discard than to repair. It is better for the economy if we keep money circulating even if some people have to take out loans to buy a new stove.

In 1970, the United States produced 4 billion tons of solid wastes which amounted to about 5 pounds (2.25 kilograms) per person. It has been estimated that by 1980 the amount will increase to 8 or 8 1/2 pounds (3.6 - 3.8 kilograms) per person. In one year, we easily discard 7 million autos, 26 billion bottles, 48 billion cans, 15 million tons of glass, and 35 million tons of wood fiber.

Unfortunately, when we discard, our means of disposal damage the environment. Open dumps are unsightly, smelly, and breeding grounds of rodents and cockroaches—both potential disease carriers. Even sanitary land fills leave much to be desired, though the garbage is covered with soil and eventually, the dump can be completely filled and converted to a recreational area. Regardless of which kind of land disposal is used, the environment is altered and the natural area is destroyed. Too often solid waste disposal facilities are located on the shore of a lake or in a marsh. The rubbish is usually carried into the water by the wind and the liquid waste leaches into the water contaminating it with undesirable solid, chemical and bacteria wastes. Moreover, the land or marsh is destroyed, never to be regained.

Incineration is another method of solid waste disposal. This method also alters the environment because the waste gases and particles pollute the air. Efforts are being made, however, to improve this method. Another disadvantage to incineration is that when materials are burned, the raw materials go off as smoke and are not returned to the soil. Dumps do provide the chance for some things to decay and return important materials to the land.

Much of what is manufactured today is not *biodegradable*—that is, it will not decay or rust with time. Animal wastes, dead plants and animals, wood, paper, cardboard, tin cans, and so on will break down. Most plastics, tires, and aluminum cans do not break down at all or they take a very long time to do so. Plastic garbage bags are used more and more, and although they reduce the cost of collection, they add to the waste problem. Recently, though, plastic garbage bags have been developed that will burn and change into carbon dioxide and water rather than into poisonous gases as is the case with the other plastics.

Try to impress upon your students that litter and garbage are aesthetically undesirable and that garbage, if not disposed of properly, can be dangerous to their health.

Activity 1:   DETERMINING THE KINDS OF SOLID WASTES

MATERIALS (per student)

pencil and paper

METHODS

1. Make a chart and list the materials you think you would be throwing away. Categorize them into large groups: paper, metal, plastic, wood, glass, ceramic, cloth, food, other.
2. Each day, tally the number of materials you discard in each category.
3. Add up the total number of materials you discard each day.
4. What kinds of solid wastes do you discard?
5. What solid waste do you discard most often?
6. What happens to the waste materials after you discard them?

Activity 2:   DETERMINING HOW MUCH SOLID WASTES ARE DISCARDED

MATERIALS (per student)

average size garbage can
spring scale or bathroom scale

METHODS

1. Weigh a clean empty garbage can either on a bathroom scale, or tie twine on each handle and attach the twine to a spring scale. Record_____.
2. Fill the can with waste as you normally would.
3. Weigh the can again full of garbage. Record_____.
4. Subtract the weight of the can (#1) from the weight of the can plus the garbage (#3) to obtain the weight of the garbage. Record_____.
5. Check to see when the garbage is collected on your street or block and count the number of cans that are put out to be emptied. Record_____.

6. Multiply the number of cans by the weight of your own garbage calculated above (#4). Record_____. This will give you the approximate amount of garbage produced by your neighborhood per collection day. If garbage is collected only once a week, the total amount you determined would be for one week. How much garbage would your neighbors discard in one year? Where is your refuse taken?

Activity 3:   DETERMINING WHICH SOLID WASTES ARE BIODEGRADABLE

MATERIALS (per class)

balance or scale
magnifying glass
several large seedling flats filled with soil
watering can
various solid waste materials: metal, paper plastic, wood, glass, ceramic, cloth, food, etc.
several sticks and labels

METHODS

1. Select a variety of materials and weigh each one separately. Record_____.
2. Bury the materials under the soil in the school yard or in seedling flats and label them.
3. Sprinkle the soil once or twice a week to simulate rain if the materials are left indoors.
4. After several weeks, remove them one by one and examine each material carefully with a magnifying glass. What do you observe? Is there any evidence of decay?
5. Gently clean off the soil. Weigh each material and record the weights_____.
   Have the objects gained or lost weight? Have they stayed the same? How would you interpret your results?
6. Return the materials to the soil and check again in another few weeks.

Activity 4:   DETERMINING WHAT HAPPENS TO SOLID WASTES WHEN THEY ARE BURNED

MATERIALS (per team of 2 or 3 students)

balance or scale
Bunsen burner, stove or hot plate
tripod
covered porcelain crucible or pan
clay triangle
tongs
various solid waste materials: metal, paper, plastic, wood, glass
ceramic, cloth, food, etc.

METHODS

1. Set up your apparatus. Place the triangle on the tripod and the crucible in it, or place a pan on a hot plate or stove.
2. Cut up one of the materials, weigh it, and place it in the crucible or pan. Cover.
3. Apply heat to the bottom. Is there smoke? Is your material turning black? Is ash forming? Does the material catch fire?
4. Record your observations.
5. Let the material cool and weigh it again. Record_____.
6. What do you conclude?
7. Repeat the above with each one of the materials.
8. What materials can be burned without causing too much damage, and which materials should perhaps be buried?

BILLBOARDS AND MILES OF CONCRETE

BACKGROUND

Since the greater number of families today are not agricultural, their daily needs for food and work must be supplied by business and industry. There must be grocery stores and restaurants where they can buy their food. There must be stores and factories where they can earn a living. With these developments, more and more commercial areas spring up in and around the cities and towns, and competition for customers becomes keener. In order to induce the public to buy one product in preference to another, proprietors advertise. They send out brochures, put ads in the daily newspaper, hang signs in their windows, install neon lights over their doors, and erect billboards along the highways. So it follows that the greater the population, the more businesses and industries will be established, the greater the competition, the more extensive the advertising, and hence, more billboards result.

What do your students think of the billboards? Do they like them? Do they think they detract from the environment or haven't they paid any attention to them? Ask them where they see most of the billboards. Are they along country roads, main highways, or city streets? Why were these locations selected? What are the rulings for advertising in this manner in your locality? Can anyone erect a billboard anywhere he chooses? Have your students perform the following activity to answer some of these questions.

Activity 1:   THE STUDY OF BILLBOARDS

MATERIALS (per team of 2 or 3 students)

local and state zoning ordinances for advertising
camera
map of area
notebook and pencil

MATERIALS (per class)

large sheet	glue and straight pins
woolen yarn	cardboard
needle and thread	marking pens

METHODS

1. Take a ride or walk around town and photograph each billboard you find. Mark the location on your map. Record the name of the advertising company that owns the billboard.
2. Compare your information with other teams in your class.
3. Construct a mural representing your local map. Use a sheet for the background and woolen yarn for the streets. Sew the yarn in place. With a marking pen, write the street names on cardboard labels and pin or glue them in place. Glue your

photographs of the billboards along the streets where they are actually located on the original map.

4. While some students are working on the mural, a team of 2 or 3 students can visit the Town or City Hall and consult with someone in the Town Planning and Zoning Office regarding advertising regulations for billboards. Look up and read the appropriate ordinances.

5. A second team can write to your congressmen and ask for copies of the Highway Beautification Act. Also ask them to bring you up-to-date on the Senate bill (S1442) authorizing $15 million for pilot programs to remove billboards from highways.

6. Another team can contact the company or companies that own the billboards and ask them how land and permits are obtained for this purpose, and also, how they contact customers. What would happen to them financially if they were no longer allowed to erect billboards?

7. Still another team can call, or better, visit the companies that are advertising on the billboards. Ask them in fact, if they think that this kind of advertising is really profitable. Would they agree to not advertise in this manner if all the other companies likewise agreed?

8. Gather all the information together and discuss it with the whole class. Should billboards remain or be removed? Are the advertisers complying with local zoning ordinances? Are they detracting from the beauty of the area? What are the economic implications if all billboards were to be removed? What Federal legislation is now in force? What action, if any, can or should be taken by the class?

By now your students should realize that billboards can be found almost anywhere automobiles travel, and that the greater concentration of them is in dense commercial areas with miles and miles of concrete! As the population grows and becomes more mobile, more buildings and highways are constructed. If the land in the United States were divided, each American would have only 11 acres. It is predicted that by 2,000, there will be only 7 acres per person. Although about half (49%) of our land is farmland, much of it is not being used. Forests cover 26.4%, wilderness areas, parks and recreation areas take up another 4.4% and the Federal government owns 34%. The cities of the country only occupy 8% of the land and the majority of the 200 million people reside in the cities. It is expected that within the next 30 years or so, the population will grow to 300 million, and the additional 100 million will still live in and around the cities. This means that there will be an even greater need for destroying the land and filling it in for buildings and roads. Even if new communities were established, buildings would still have to be erected, and highways would still have to be constructed to provide access to these towns and cities.

Obtain a map of your locality from your Town Plan and Zoning Office that shows the residential, commercial, industrial, recreational and open space areas and have your students follow the procedures below.

Activity 1:   POPULATION GROWTH AND LAND USE

MATERIALS (per class)

copy of local Planning Map
copy of the Highway Beautification Act (S 2084 - PL 89-285)
copy of the National Land-Use Policy Act (S 3354)

METHODS

1. Write to your Congressman and ask for copies of the National Land-Use Act and also ask him to bring you up-to-date on this bill.
2. Obtain a planning map of your town showing the residential, industrial, commercial, recreational, and open space areas from the Town Plan and Zoning Office.
3. From your map, determine the total number of acres comprising your town. Then find out what percentage of land is being used by business and industry, and what is used for residents, recreation and open space. What occupies the most land?
4. If the population were to increase by 50% within the next 30 years, where would you put the people? Would it be better to construct single family dwellings or multiple family dwellings?
5. If the population increases, the demand for homes and jobs will also increase. Where and how would you expand the commercial and business areas? If you live on a farm, dairy, or cattle area, what then? Can you follow the recommendations of the National Land-Use Policy Act?

"LISTENING" TO NOISE POLLUTION

BACKGROUND

Some people are wild about rock and roll music, boogy-woogie and jazz. To others, this kind of music is nothing but noise and can be terribly irritating to the listener. The sound of a fog horn coming in over the ocean can be soothing and restful. To others, it can elicit fear and concern for loved ones at sea. The roar of a roller coaster can be exciting and terrifying at the same time. Birds singing in the morning can be a pleasant welcome to a new day while to the person who wants to sleep, it can be noise. So we see that depending upon our experiences and likes and dislikes, sounds can be classified as noise and at other times as something pleasant, or even, music.

When we refer to noise as an environmental pollutant, noise is defined as sound so loud it can cause deafness and illness. Noise level is measured in units called *decibels*. The threshold of pain has been placed at between 130 and 150 decibels. Hearing loss can occur as a result of continuous exposure to sound levels of 85 decibels and above. Today's teenagers have poor hearing mainly because they believe their stereo sets must be played at high volume though many of the musical groups already exceed the safe sound level when they use amplifiers. Many men and women working in offices and factories also suffer from loss of hearing when exposed to continuous excessive noises.

We are constantly aware of noise around us and many of us seek refuge away from the hubbub of the city, from the noise of cars and trucks, the squeal of brakes, the honking of horns, the shrill sound of the ambulance or police car siren, the whine of a fire engine, the pounding of typewriters, the pounding of a jackhammer, and the roar of machines in a factory or jet aircraft. Everyone needs peace and quiet, a time to think, a time to listen to one's inner self and nature. Don't forget that your students too, need time to think and to listen.

According to the American Association for the Advancement of Science, noise pollution causes much more than deafness. It can cause people to become nervous and tense, irritable and frustrated. When noise interferes with sleep, some individuals have developed ulcers or high blood pressure, and the loss of peace of mind has brought on heart attacks. As blood vessels constrict, researchers have found that higher cholesterol levels result. Noise can cause seizures in epileptics, and it affects the autonomic nervous system which controls the heart, blood vessels, muscles, and glands. Research on rats reveals that noise can trigger the production of hormones that cause the amount of salt and water in their bodies to increase, making them ill. Additionally, it has been found that a pregnant woman produces hormones under stress of noise that can affect the unborn child adversely. The unborn fetus also responds to outside noises and again, experiments on rats reveal that such offspring learn more slowly and are often emotionally unstable.

Thus, we see that noise is not only annoying but also dangerous. To explore the level of sound you and your students are exposed to each day, conduct the following activity.

Activity 1: MEASURING SOUND LEVELS

MATERIALS (per class)

decibel meter or tape recorder   graph paper
chart paper   meter stick
                                   notebook and pencil

METHODS

1. Measure the size of your classroom. Record in your notebook.
2. Make a list of everything in your room, e.g., the number and size of the windows, the shades, bulletin boards, chalkboards, desks chairs, benches, etc.
3. Describe the room and the materials which make up the floor, walls, ceiling, furniture, etc. Do you have a rug on the floor? Are the walls plaster? Is the ceiling made of acoustical material? Is the furniture plastic, metal, wood? Are there shades and drapes at the windows?
4. Obtain a decibel meter from the music, maintenance, speech and hearing, or science departments. (They cost about $40.00.) If none is available use a tape recorder and record the levels registered on the intensity gauge. Leave the volume on normal.
5. Using the decibel meter (or tape recorder) record the noise level in the classroom during various activities such as during class discussions, independent study or laboratory work. Do this for one week and record on a large chart. At the end of the week, plot the number of decibels on graph paper for each activity.
6. When is the class the noisiest? What is the decibel range in your room from lowest to highest? How can you cut down on the noise? What changes can or should you make in the room?
7. Repeat the above with other rooms in the school and compare the graphs. What room is the noisiest in the school? When is it noisiest in the halls?
8. Prepare a report based on your investigations and present a copy to the Principal, the Superintendent, and to the Chairman of the Board of Education. Be sure to include specific date and recommendations for improvement.

PESTICIDES

BACKGROUND

Since Rachel Carson's book, *Silent Spring,* was published in 1962, pesticides and their effects have received much public attention. Of all the pesticides, DDT has been given the most notoriety. DDT, or dichloro-diphenyl-trichloroethane, kills all insects whether harmful or not. Obviously, this would be a serious threat to food chains and webs. If, by chance, insects do survive being sprayed by DDT, their offspring are naturally immune to DDT. It has also been found that organisms tend to absorb DDT and pass this concentration of pesticide on to another organism in a higher trophic level. This means that the top predator receives all the DDT absorbed and transferred from all the prey below it in a food chain. Scientists have discovered very high concentrations of DDT in eagle eggs, for instances. DDT has been blamed for the inability of birds to lay thick shelled eggs. The shells are so thin that they often break when the mother bird sits on them. It is believed therefore, that DDT is responsible for the scarcity of the bald eagle and the osprey.

DDT is classified as a *hard* or *persistent* pesticide because it does not break down readily to form non-toxic compounds, and it remains in the environment for many years. DDT can remain toxic for 20 years. Scientists took mud from an estuary that had been sprayed with DDT 10 years before and placed some fiddler crabs with it. The DDT was still toxic and killed the crabs. DDT will get into the ocean and other water resources. It effects photosynthesis in algae which will eventually alter the amount of oxygen produced. Man drinks DDT in water and ingests it with food. It is absorbed in fatty tissue and has been found in urine and in the milk of nursing mothers. The potential danger to humans is not really known, but indeed, it is there.

To say that all pesticides should be banned is a bit drastic. Even DDT has its advantages. DDT was given credit for the elimination of typhoid fever and malaria during World War II and since then has saved crops from millions of dollars of insect damage. Other pesticides are more specific and are termed, *insecticides, fungicides, herbicides,* and *germicides.* These chemicals are helpful if used properly and can control pests and disease causing organisms. Sprays are used on shade trees, orchards, crops, gardens, household pests and the like.

Pesticides are classified as *non-persistent, moderately persistent* and *permanent.* The classification is based on how long the chemicals last in the environment. *Non-persistent* pesticides last from several days to approximately a month. *Moderately persistent* pesticides last 1 to 18 months. *Persistent* or *hard* pesticides last for many years. *Permanent* pesticides remain indefinitely. The most important groups are the latter two. The persistent pesticides, such as DDT, are the chlorinated hydrocarbons and also include aldrin, dieldrin, andrin, heptachlor, and toxaphene. The permanent ones contain a base of heavy elements such as arsenic, lead and mercury.

A thorough investigation of pesticides can be made by your students. Contact your state's agricultural experiment station, your state representatives and local garden shops for more information.

Activity 1:   AN INVESTIGATION INTO PESTICIDES

MATERIALS (per student or team of 2 or 3 students)

information on pesticides
reference books
local, state and federal regulations

METHODS

1. As a start, look up pesticides in the libary and review research papers until you decide on which class of pesticides or which specific problem you wish to concentrate on.
2. Define your problem or topic—state it as clearly and as precisely as possible.
3. Read as much as you can on the topic. Write to the U.S. Environmental Protection Agency and to your state Department of Environmental Protection and ask for copies of bills or laws that pertain to your topic.
4. Talk to resource people in local garden shops, tree nurseries, florists, nearby colleges and universities, and the state's agriculture experiment station.
5. Take notes on what you read and on your interviews with experts. Write up your report and in doing so consider the ecological, social, economic, and political aspects of the problem.
6. Include recommendations on how the problems can be controlled or solved.
7. Devise alternative plans of action and predict possible consequences to these plans.
8. Discuss your findings as a whole class and determine if any plans are worth implementing. If so, work with other departments in your school to carry them out and share your information with your local Conservation Commission or environmental protection agent.

RADIATION

BACKGROUND

Another hazard created by progress is atomic radiation. Like pesticides, atomic energy is not all bad—only some types of radiation are harmful. As a teacher you are already aware of medical uses of radiation in the location and treatment of disease by using radioactive isotopes, and in the use of X-rays in search of broken bones, decayed teeth, lung lesions and so on. Nuclear energy is being used as fuel to generate electric power and other uses of nuclear fuels are being explored everyday.

Where does radiation come from? Is it only from medical uses, power plants and bombs? What is radiation?

Radiation can be classified into three types: *ionizing radiation, background radiation,* and *man-made radiation.* Ionizing radiation is any radiation that displaces electrons (negatively charged particles) from atoms or molecules, causing ions (charged atoms) to form. Background radiation, or natural radiation, is what is naturally present in the atmosphere. This radiation comes from cosmic rays which bombard the atmosphere from outer space, and naturally occurring radioactive elements found in mineral deposits, water, and living things. Man-made radiation is that which is released when man uses energy in the form of radioactive tracer elements and X-rays in industry and medicine, and is radiation released during nuclear tests in the atmosphere.

Ionizing radiation consists of *alpha, beta* and *gamma rays,* and short-wave *ultra violet light.* Alpha rays are streams of positively charged particles, or Helium nuclei, emitted by radioactive elements with a penetrating power of 5 to 10 centimeters of air and can be stopped by a piece of paper. Alpha particles are not dangerous unless they enter the blood stream through an open wound or are ingested with radioactive food.

Beta rays are streams of negatively charged particles emitted from a nucleus during radioactive decay with a penetrating power of 2 to 10 meters of air and can be stopped by a thin sheet of metal. Beta radiation can cause skin burns and the beta-emitters are harmful if they enter the body of animals.

Gamma rays have no charge and are a form of electromagnetic radiation of short-wave length and high energy. (*Electromagnetic* radiation consists of electric and magnetic waves that travel at the speed of light such as visible light, radio waves, and X-rays.) Gamma rays are similar to X-rays but come from nuclei during fission (splitting of nuclei) and usually have greater energy. Gamma rays are more penetrating than alpha and beta rays and can be stopped only by 2.413 kilometers of air, by 93 centimeters of concrete or by 31 centimeters of lead. Gamma rays can seriously damage cells, chromosomes and genes. They can induce mutations, cause cancer, kill cells and eventually, the whole organism.

Short-wave (frequencies between 10^{16} and 10^{17} cycles per second) ultraviolet radiation is more energetic than visible light (frequencies between 1014 and 1015 cycles per second). Ultraviolet radiation is also a form of magnetic radiation but it is not very penetrating. Continuous exposure, however, (as many sunbathers know) will cause a reddening of the skin, stimulate the production of pigment and if exposure persists, skin cancer can result. Ultraviolet radiation will sometimes interfere with replication of chromosomes and will stimulate chemical changes. One good aspect of ultraviolet radiation is that it breaks down some steroids to form vitamin D for strong bones and teeth.

Background radiation consists of radiation from naturally occurring radioactive elements such as uranium, radium, and plutonium, and lesser radioactive elements found in water and mineral deposits; also from some carbon and potassium atoms in animals. This radiation is primarily in the form of alpha, beta and gamma rays. Background radiation also consists of cosmic rays. Cosmic rays are streams of positively charged particles, predominantly hydrogen nuclei. Cosmic rays originate outside the earth's atmosphere and have very high energies. Some cosmic rays are absorbed by the atmosphere and other rays are deflected toward the poles by the earth's magnetic field. Thus, the intensity of cosmic radiation varies from place to place.

Man contributed to the background radiation, and hence, to radiation pollution, when Wilhelm Roentgen discovered X-rays in 1895. Eventually, these were used in industry and in medicine for medical diagnosis and therapy. When radioactivity was discovered in 1896, radioactive materials were brought into the laboratories to be studied. Later, in 1934, scientists discovered they could transform nonradioactive elements into radioactive elements and they were also used by physicians and researchers. In 1945, the nuclear bomb was developed, and whenever fission occurs with plutonium or uranium resulting in a nuclear explosion, there is intense radiation of gamma rays. There is also a residual of other radioactive elements. These particles remain in the atmospheric currents, circulate over the earth, and eventually descend as radioactive *fallout*.

Ever since man bombed Hiroshima and Nagasaki in 1945, we have been able to study the long term effects of high-energy radiation. Those who survived the bombing suffered from *radiation sickness.* Some people eventually died from it while others recovered slowly. High-energy radiation damages the cells and the mechanism for cell division and reproduction. Sometimes the cells are killed directly and other times the delicate structure of the genes and chromosomes are damaged preventing cell division. If the cells are those needed for growth and repair, their inability to divide could be very damaging. On the other hand, if they are not, normal cells can often take over their function. If chromosomes are damaged only slightly, cell division and/or reproduction of a new organism may result but the offspring are mutations. Such disorders cause leukemia, tumors, skin cancer, or deformed children, animals and plants.

Although many experiments with radioactive materials can be performed safely in a laboratory, you should demonstrate the proper techniques for handling "hot" (radioactive) materials and give the students practice with nonradioactive materials first. The following activities are not dangerous and still provide some experience with radiation.

Activity 1:   OBSERVING SUBATOMIC PARTICLES

MATERIALS (per class)

cloud   chamber with radioactive source (obtained from most science supply houses)
paper and pencil
block of dry ice

METHODS

1. Set up your cloud chamber on a block of dry ice according to the instructions from the manufacturer.
2. Do not put in any radioactive source at first. Observe for 5 minutes. What do you see? Make a drawing of your observations. Where do these tracks come from?
3. Put in various radioactive source materials, one at a time, and observe. Draw what you see. How do these tracks compare to the background radiation tracks above? Are all the tracks you observe the same?
4. Compare your observations with the descriptions below.

Background radiation tracks are thin and wobble because they are traveling at a slow speed and are not very heavy (mostly beta particles and cosmic rays).

Alpha radiation tracks are straight and thick because they are traveling at a high speed from a radioactive source and are heavy.

Beta radiation tracks are straight but thinner and longer than the alpha tracks because they too are traveling fast from a radioactive source. Beta particles are not as heavy as alpha particles which explains why they are less dense.

Activity 2:   DETECTING BACKGROUND RADIATION

MATERIALS (per class)

Geiger-Muller Radiation Counters (obtained from your local Civil Defense Department)
chart paper
graph paper
notebook and paper

METHODS

1. Read the instructions on how to use the Geiger counters and record the types and what kind of radiation they measure. (Probably alpha, beta and gamma radiation.)
2. Make a chart so you can record the number of counts in 10 second intervals and counts per minute.
3. Begin counting and recording for 20 minutes. Count the clicks you hear in a 10 second period. Particles enter the counter at random and therefore, you may get 6 or 7 counts during one interval and perhaps none during another.
4. When the 20 minutes are up, add all the 10-second interval counts together for the total. Record_____. What is the average count per minute?_____. Graph your results.
5. Repeat the above with the other counters. What type of radiation is most prevalent in the room?_____.
   What is the ratio of alpha, beta and gamma radiation present? _____.
6. Taking one counter at a time, try to locate the major source of radioactivity of that type in the room. Record_____. What kinds of material appear to contain some radioactive elements?_____. Would you say the room is heavily contaminated or polluted with radiation?

RECYCLING—BENEFICIAL OR NOT?

BACKGROUND

In previous sections, your students have learned that the process of recycling occurs in nature. They will recall that metabolic wastes in biological systems, as in a food web, are returned to the soil for plants to use again. Water is recycled. It evaporates and falls again to the land as rain or snow. Doesn't it seem sensible then, to reuse man-made wastes? The reprocessing of waste materials for reuse is also called *recycling*. These waste materials that can be recycled are plastics, metals, paper and glass. Other wastes that are more difficult to dispose of and just as difficult to recycle are old tires and pesticides.

We are not too concerned about wet garbage, such as food scraps and wet paper, because these materials are biodegradable and decomposers will eventually break them down in sanitary landfills. We are concerned though about the raw materials leaching into the dump area and being lost to a viable ecosystem. By composting these materials in a corner of one's backyard, these raw materials will be recycled through the food chains and webs.

Plastics pose another problem because most of them are not biodegradable and will persist in the environment. Neither can they be burned safely due to the poisonous gases produced. Some of them when burned produce corrosive hydrochloric acid and thus pollute the air. The majority of plastics don't burn at all but melt instead, and foul the grates of the incinerators. Plastics are flooding the market in the form of packaging material to the extent that 3% (by weight) of our packaging material is plastic. We have plastic cups, plastic bags, plastic wrap, plastic containers, plastic trays, and so on. Recently, reseachers have found that the polyvinyl chloride (PVC) plastic containers slowly leach plasticizer into protein substances—that is, substances such as meat, or blood in blood banks absorb the plasticizer from the plastic container. Evidence of accumulated quantities have been found in the liver, spleen, lungs, and abominal fat of patients transfused with blood stored in these plastic bags.

Two ways to recycle plastics would be: first, to develop more plastics that are biodegradable; and second, to remold used plastics into something new. If all milk containers, for example, were made of the same type of plastic, they could be collected together and remolded. As it is now, there are many types of plastics being used and a general collection of all would make the separation, washing, and grinding too expensive. The scientists have more work to do in this area.

Although metals make up only a small percentage of the mass of solid wastes, they still present a problem for disposal and recycling. Regardless, they must be recycled because metals are natural resources of fixed amounts, and it is estimated that within 50 years we will have used up our tin and zinc unless they are reclaimed after use. Junk automobiles present the greatest problem. It is difficult to separate the various materials of which a car is made. Cars are made of ferrous (iron) metals, copper, chrome, plastic, glass, fabric, and rubber. Steel mills and foundries make use of 6% of junk autos for the iron content but much of the other material is not reclaimed. It is still a costly process to compact, shred, and separate the materials to make them available for reuse. Additional problems arise when one considers the fluctuating scrap supply and demand, transportation costs, and changing steel production technology.

Tires present a problem all their own. They do not disintegrate in sanitary landfills and always manage to rise to the top when compaction is attempted. They cannot be incinerated because they pollute the air, nor can they be recycled. Tires are not just made of natural or synthetic rubber, but plastic, nylon and steel. Trying to separate them into their parts would be a difficult and expensive task. Some hope for the use of old tires has been envisioned though, by the Bureau of Solid Waste Management and the Fish and Wildlife Service. These federal departments have investigated the possibility of using the tires to establish artificial reefs and fish havens along the Atlantic coast. Tires are set in sandy areas to provide sea life with some protection and spawning grounds. If continued success is realized, many useless tires could be turned into beneficial functional devices.

Beverage containers, of which cans are a part, comprise 3.9% of refuse collected, and this amount is increasing. Cans for food goods and beverages are made of steel and tin alloy or of aluminum. If the steel could be extracted, it would sell as scrap metal for about $20.00 per ton. The tin would eventually rust but, as stated before, it should be reclaimed since the United States has already used more than one quarter of its total mineral supply. Aluminum does not readily disintegrate and should be reclaimed and recycled. Some companies have paid 10c per pound (453 grams) for used aluminum.

Our greatest waste material is paper but fortunately, paper and paper products are biodegradable. Paper can also be easily recycled and used again as boxes, cartons and stationery. Obviously, trees are sacrificed to make paper, and although trees can be replanted, by recycling 1 ton of paper, seventeen trees can be saved. As it is, Americans consume 430 pounds or 195.5 kilograms of paper yearly.

Of this amount only approximately 19% is actually recycled. The rest finds it way to the incinerator to pollute the air, to the dump, or is left on the roadsides and at beaches and parks as litter.

Glass is nonbiodegradable but can be ground up and used as filler insulation, and in road-building material. The problem in recylcing it is in collecting and removing plastic and metal parts from the glass, and in separating it by colors. The returnable bottle, apparently for economic reasons, is a thing of the past. It is cheaper to make new glass bottles than to retrieve, wash, and refill old ones.

In some cases, there is evidence that recycling is beneficial and indeed, sometimes necessary if we are to continue to have certain materials. In other cases, the cost is prohibitive or the technology for recycling has not been perfected to make the reprocessing profitable. Some states, such as Connecticut, have devised a long term plan to recover resources and the authorities claim that recycling can be practical, feasible and economically advantageous. Dan W. Lufkin, former Connecticut State Commissioner of the Department of Environmental Protection, and his committee have suggested that much can be gained if the total community cooperates in the fight against the solid waste crises. In a state-wide system, they propose there should be centers for collection, separation, materials recovery, and processing. These centers should be located according to population density so that people would be living within one waste shed or another and their refuse would be sent to the collection center within their own waste shed. With this approach and long range planning and projections, economic benefits, recovery of our resources and overall environmental improvement should result.

Perhaps your students would like to become involved in some recycling activities. What is your school doing now? What is your community doing about the solid waste crises and recycling? Has your state or district made any effort to encourage recycling? Provide opportunities for your students to investigate the status of recycling in your area. Perhaps they may feel a need to join a community action group or to start a recycling drive or center of their own. Find out which manufacturers or businesses in your area are willing to cooperate. Have the students contact a local group of organic farmers to discuss the advantages of organic gardening and composting. As an outgrowth, the students might want to try the following activities.

Activity 1: COMPOSTING

MATERIALS (per class)

small plot of land 1.86 meters x 1.86 meters or

large refuse bin
references on composting

METHODS

1. Select an obscure section of the school yard away from the building for a site for a compost pile.
2. Read about composting and contact resource people in the area to learn more about the advantages of composting and how to build a compost pile.
3. Select a team of 2 or 3 students to present your proposal to build a compost pile in the school yard to the principal of the school.
4. If the principal grants you permission, work out the details on separating and collecting the food wastes with the person in charge of the cafeteria.
5. Stake out and fence off the dumping area and erect a sign in front of it so no one will disturb the plot. If you prefer, use a large refuse container instead of dumping on the ground.
6. Send another delegation to speak to the maintenance department and arrange to have them dump grass cuttings and brush trimmings into the compost pile. (Addition of animal wastes, due to their high nitrogen content, will speed up the decomposing process too.)
7. Each day, dump the food wastes onto the pile until you have filled the designated area. Stir it once a month with a shovel or long pole.
8. Observe what happens to your compost each month. Describe the changes that have taken place. It will take from three to six months for your compost to decompose into a rich, natural fertilizer. How long does your compost pile take to decompose?
9. When your compost has broken down, take some of the runoff water from it and water 2 or 3 plants. Take 2 or 3 more identical plants and water them with ordinary water. Do you see a difference? Explain your results. Do you think composting is worthwhile?
10. Contact your local Organic Garden Association or write to your state or national association. Learn how to garden the organic way and use your decomposed compost accordingly. If you wish, write to Educational Services Division, Rodale Press, Incorporated, Emmaus, Pennsylvania 18049 for more information on organic gardening.

PEOPLE, PEOPLE AND MORE PEOPLE

BACKGROUND

In 1830, there were 1 billion people in the world. In 1970, the number had risen to 3.5 billion. By 2000, there will be 7 billion persons, and an estimated 14 billion has been predicted by 2015. The planet earth is reaching its capacity to support life and if it should, what then? Can we escape to another planet and likewise, pollute that too? Is man, in fact, the most endangered species of all and is he irreversibly destined to become extinct because of his own short-sightedness? All the ills of the cities and all our environmental problems are caused by nothing more than too many people in competition for too little food, too few goods, too little space, and unconsciously too, for a limited amount of natural resources of which air and water are of prime importance. The population is growing at a rate of 2% a year and today, more than 1 billion human beings are suffering from malnutrition and undernourishment. How can we possibly keep up with the demand for food with shrinking space and natural resources?

In the United States, every nine seconds a baby is born. It has been calculated that each child will consume in his life time 9 tons of milk, 5 1/2 tons of wheat, 5 1/2 tons of meat, 37 thousand gallons of gasoline, and 56 million gallons of water. Americans consume about half of the world's resources yet comprise only 6% of the world's population. This consumption presents a tremendous drain on our natural resources, and overpopulation threatens the possibility for children to grow up as healthy and contributing human beings.

If we are to preserve the sanctity of life, people must grow up with dignity. Slums, poverty, and starvation have deprived millions of people of human dignity. Research and experience has shown that overcrowded conditions breed frustration, abnormal behavior, and violence, or dullness and indifference. Human beings have the intelligence to control their own destinies and to predict disaster and yet, we are often blind to the realization that we too are a part of the stream of life and must take responsibility for our own actions. We can no longer ignore the fact that what we do does affect the whole. We must realize that the "it-doesn't-apply-to-me attitude" must be abandoned for the "I-am-responsible-too" attitude.

Is the picture really all doom and gloom? Will man allow himself to overpopulate to the extent that he will self-destruct? Man's genius has split the atom and sent men to the moon. Man has moved mountains and changed the weather. Does this sound like a species that will destroy itself? On the other hand, man has allowed the environmental problems to build up; he has allowed men to fight one another; he has allowed nations to wage war.

As a teacher you have the responsibility to discuss the pros and cons of overpopulation with your students. Present the facts so that they can develop their own code of ethics and sense of values. Do not inflict your prejudices on them. How do they feel about our destiny? What decisions will man make and how might they each contribute to the salvation of mankind?

The nature of man and the will of God are an enigma. According to some authorities there will be room and food for an increased world population if man approaches the environmental problems sensibly. Education then, as in all things, must play a vital role in bringing knowledge of the truth, of what is good, of what is beautiful and desirable, to the youth of today. We must give them the tools to construct new knowledge and to build on the old. If through education, we can change human behavior and our way of thinking and doing, and if we try to nurture within our youth brotherly love, respect for human dignity, and consideration for the needs and rights of others, man will be sustained.

GLOSSARY

alpha particle — radioactive material which is made up of 2 protons and 2 neutrons, and therefore, is identical in structure with a helium atom nucleus. It is not harmful unless the alpha emitter enters the body.

beta particle — in general a negatively charged particle emitted from the nucleus of a radioactive atom having the characteristics of an electron. Positively charged beta particles are called positrons. Can cause burns if in contact with skin or are ingested.

biodegradable — will decay or rust with time and eventually disappear into the soil.

decibels — a unit used to measure the intensity (volume) of sound.

gamma rays — high energy, nuclear particles having no charge, found in the short wavelength of the electromagnetic field; are very penetrating and hence harmful to animal life.

isotope — atoms of the same element existing in different forms, that is, they have the same atomic number but different atomic mass—in other words, the nuclei of these isotopes have the same number of protons but differing numbers of neutrons.

radioisotope — radioactive isotope

BIBLIOGRAPHY

Andrews, William A. *A Guide to the Study of Environmental Pollution.* Englewood Cliffs, New Jersey: Prentice-Hall, Inc., 1972.

Asimov, Isaac, and Theodosius Dobshansky. *The Genetic Effects of Radiation.* Understanding the Atom Series. United States Atomic Energy Commission, 1968.

Blaustein, Elliott H. *Anit-Pollution Labs.* New York: Sentinel Book Publishers, Inc., 1972.

Calliet, Greg M., Paulette Y. Setzer, and Milton S. Love. *Everyone's Guide to Ecological Living.* New York: Macmillan Company, 1971.

Comar, Cyril L. *Fallout from Nuclear Tests.* Understanding the Atom Series. United States Atomic Energy Commission, 1967.

Congressional Quarterly. *Man's Control of the Environment.* 1735 K Street N.W., Washington, D.C., August 1970.

Fox, Charles H. *Radioactive Wastes.* Understanding the Atom Series. United States Atomic Energy Commission, 1967.

O'Donnell, Patrick A., and Charles W. Lavaroni. *Noise Pollution.* Reading, Massachusetts: Addison-Wesley Publishing Company, Inc., 1971.

Pauline, Lawrence J., and Howard Weishaus. *Ecology: Man's Relationship to His Environment.* New York: Oxford Book Company, 1971.

Stollberg, Robert, and Faith Fitch Hill. *Physics Fundamentals and Frontiers.* Boston: Houghton-Mifflin Company, 1965.

Storin, Diane. *Investigating Air, Land, and Water Pollution.* Bronxville, New York: Pawnee Publishing Company, Inc., 1971.

Wentworth, D.F., J.K. Couchman, J.C. MacBean, and A. Stecher. *Pollution-Examining Your Environment.* Minneapolis, Minnestoa: Mine Publications, 1971.

Appendix

PLAY DOUGH

1 cup or 0.275 liter flour
1 cup or 0.275 liter salt
1 tablespoon or 14.7 milliliters powdered alum

Mix dry ingredients together. Add slowly one half cup or 0.138 liter of water and mix thoroughly. Food coloring may be added if you prefer color to the bland color of this mixture. The dough may be kept soft and workable for a long time if it is stored in a tightly covered jar or can.

THE METRIC SYSTEM

LINEAR MEASURE

10 millimeters	= 1 centimeter
10 centimeters	= 1 decimeter
10 decimeters	= 1 meter
10 meters	= 1 decameter
10 decameters	= 1 hectometer
10 hectometers	= 1 kilometer

SQUARE MEASURE

100 square millimeters	= 1 square centimeter
100 square centimeters	= 1 square decimeter
100 square decimeters	= 1 square meter
100 square meters	= 1 square decameter
100 square decameters	= 1 square hectometer
100 square hectometers	= 1 square kilometer

LIQUID MEASURE

10 milliliters	= 1 centiliter
10 centiliters	= 1 deciliter
10 deciliters	= 1 liter

10 liters	= 1 decaliter
10 decaliters	= 1 hectoliter
10 hectoliters	= 1 kiloliter
1000 milliliters	= 1 liter

MASS

10 milligrams	= 1 centigram
10 centigrams	= 1 decigram
10 decigrams	= 1 gram
10 grams	= 1 decagram
10 decagrams	= 1 hectogram
10 hectograms	= 1 kilogram
10 kilograms	= 1 quintal
10 quintals	= 1 ton

CONVERSION OF ENGLISH UNITS TO METRIC UNITS

LINEAR

1 inch	= 25.4001 millimeters
1 inch	= 2.54001 centimeters
1 foot	= 0.304 meter
1 yard	= 0.914 meter
1 mile	= 1.609 kilometers

SQUARE

1 square inch	= 645.16 square millimeters
1 square inch	= 6.4516 square centimeters
1 square foot	= 0.092 square meter
1 square yard	= 0.836 square meter
1 square mile	= 2.59 square kilometers
1 acre	= 0.404 hectare

CUBE

1 cubic inch	= 16,387.2 cubic millimeters
1 cubit foot	= 0.0283 cubic meter
1 cubic yard	= 0.764 cubic meter

VOLUME

1 U.S. liquid ounce	= 29.573 milliliters

1 U.S. liquid quart	= 0.946 liter
1 U.S. liquid gallon	= 3.785 liters
1 U.S. dry quart	= 1.1012 liters
1 U.S. peck	= 8.809 liters
1 U.S. bushel	= 0.352 hectoliter

CONVERSION OF METRIC UNITS TO ENGLISH UNITS

LINEAR

1 millimeter	= 0.0393 inch
1 centimeter	= 0.3937 inch
1 meter	= 3.280 feet
1 kilometer	= 0.621 mile

VOLUME

4.9 milliliters	= 1 teaspoon
14.7 milliliters	= 1 tablespoon
30 milliliters	= 1 fluid ounce
1 liter	= 1.056 U.S. liquid quart

MASS

| 1 gram | = 0.035 avoirdupois ounce |
| 1 kilogram | = 2.204 avoirdupois pounds |

TABLE OF TRIGONOMETRIC RATIOS

Angle	Sine	Cosine	Tangent	omit		Angle	Sine	Cosine	Tangent	omit	
0	0.0000	1.0000	0.0000		90	23	0.3907	0.9205	0.4245	2.3559	67
1	0.0175	0.9998	0.0175	57.290	89	24	0.4067	0.9135	0.4452	2.2460	66
2	0.0349	0.9994	0.0349	28.636	88	25	0.4226	0.9063	0.4663	2.1445	65
3	0.0523	0.9986	0.0524	19.081	87	26	0.4384	0.8988	0.4877	2.0503	64
4	0.0698	0.9976	0.0699	14.301	86	27	0.4540	0.8910	0.5095	1.9626	63
5	0.0872	0.9962	0.0875	11.430	85	28	0.4695	0.8829	0.5317	1.8807	62
6	0.1045	0.9945	0.1051	9.5144	84	29	0.4848	0.8746	0.5543	1.8040	61
7	0.1219	0.9925	0.1228	8.1443	83	30	0.5000	0.8660	0.5774	1.7321	60
8	0.1392	0.9903	0.1405	7.1154	82	31	0.5150	0.8572	0.6009	1.6643	59
9	0.1564	0.9877	0.1584	6.3138	81	32	0.5299	0.8480	0.6249	1.6003	58
10	0.1736	0.9848	0.1763	5.6713	80	33	0.5446	0.8387	0.6494	1.5399	57
11	0.1908	0.9816	0.1944	5.1446	79	34	0.5592	0.8290	0.6745	1.4826	56
12	0.2079	0.9781	0.2126	4.7046	78	35	0.5736	0.8192	0.7002	1.4281	55
13	0.2250	0.9744	0.2309	4.3315	77	36	0.5878	0.8090	0.7265	1.3764	54
14	0.2419	0.9703	0.2493	4.0108	76	37	0.6018	0.7986	0.7536	1.3270	53
15	0.2588	0.9659	0.2679	3.7321	75	38	0.6157	0.7880	0.7813	1.2799	52
16	0.2756	0.9613	0.2867	3.4874	74	39	0.6293	0.7771	0.8098	1.2349	51
17	0.2924	0.9563	0.3057	3.2709	73	40	0.6428	0.7660	0.8391	1.1918	50
18	0.3090	0.9511	0.3249	3.0777	72	41	0.6561	0.7547	0.8693	1.1504	49
19	0.3256	0.9455	0.3443	2.9042	71	42	0.6692	0.7431	0.9004	1.1106	48
20	0.3420	0.9397	0.3640	2.7475	70	43	0.6820	0.7314	0.9325	1.0724	47
21	0.3584	0.9336	0.3839	2.6051	69	44	0.6947	0.7193	0.9657	1.0355	46
22	0.3746	0.9272	0.4040	2.4751	68	45	0.7071	0.7071	1.0000	1.0000	45
	Cosine	Sine	omit	Tangent	Angle		Cosine	Sine	omit	Tangent	Angle

CENTIGRADE TO FAHRENHEIT CONVERSION

°C	°F	°C	°F	°C	°F	°C	°F
0	32	26	79	51	124	76	169
1	34	27	81	52	126	77	171
2	36	28	82	53	127	78	172
3	37	29	84	54	129	79	174
4	39	30	86	55	131	80	176
5	41	31	88	56	133	81	178
6	43	32	90	57	135	82	180
7	45	33	91	58	136	83	181
8	46	34	93	59	138	84	183
9	48	35	95	60	140	85	185
10	50	36	97	61	142	86	187
11	52	37	99	62	144	87	189
12	54	38	100	63	145	88	190
13	55	39	102	64	147	89	192
14	57	40	104	65	149	90	194
15	59	41	106	66	151	91	196
16	61	42	108	67	153	92	198
17	63	43	109	68	154	93	199
18	64	44	111	69	156	94	201
19	66	45	113	70	158	95	203
20	68	46	115	71	160	96	205
21	70	47	117	72	162	97	207
22	72	48	118	73	163	98	208
23	73	49	120	74	165	99	210
24	75	50	122	75	167	100	212
25	77						

TEMPERATURE CONVERSION FORMULAE
Fahrenheit to Centigrade: $C° = 5/9 \times F° -32$
Centigrade to Fahrenheit: $F° = 9/5 \times C° +32$

Index